D1454838

INSTRUCTOR'S MANUAL TO ACC[

FORTRAN 77
FUNDAMENTALS
AND STYLE

Walter S. Brainerd

University of New Mexico

Charles H. Goldberg

Trenton State College

Jonathan L. Gross

Columbia University

BOYD & FRASER PUBLISHING COMPANY
BOSTON

© 1985 by Walter S. Brainerd, Charles H. Goldberg, and Jonathan L. Gross. All rights reserved. No part of this work may be reproduced or used in any form or by any means—graphic, electronic, or mechanical, including photocopying, recording, taping, or information and retrieval systems—without written permission from the publisher.

Manufactured in the United States of America

ISBN 087835-146-9

10 9 8 7 6 5 4 3 2 1

PREFACE

The textbook *Fortran 77, Fundamentals and Style* is designed to be used in a one-semester course on Fortran programming and problem solving. Our objectives include the following:

- to help students achieve a good knowledge of the Fortran language
- to help students develop good techniques for solving problems, especially the top-down approach and stepwise refinement
- to provide examples of excellent programming style
- to familiarize students with the concept of programming language syntax
- to illustrate how computers are used to solve practical problems

    The preface to the text mentions a few additional abjectives, and there isn't much point in repeating or rephrasing here any more of what we already wrote there, so we won't.

About the Section Previews in the Text

The section previews are what we use a high-level guidelines to prepare lectures when we teach the course ourselves. Although most beginning students will skip over them in a first reading, the section previews are quite valuable to students when they reread or review.

About This Instructor's Manual

For the most part, the text is written for the students. This instructor's manual is written for an instructor to use in preparing lectures, in designing examinations, and in whatever other ways seem suitable.

You are going to find some unusual points of view in this instructor's manual. We dare to do the forbidden: we advocate our personal viewpoint on pedagogy. Basically, we know that if students get bored, they don't learn as much as if they are interested.

Thoroughness is only one aspect of effective teaching. Don't be afraid to be intentionally entertaining. An instructor's classroom performance is measured by results—how much and how well your students learn—not by the degree of adherence to pedagogical orthodoxy. The text itself is consummately thorough, which takes some of the pressure off you; your students can read all the details in the text.

In this instructor's manual, we have tried to go beyond throughness. It contains materials and suggestions to help you with the other parts of effective teaching, sometimes including entertainment.

We know perfectly well that there are many effective teaching styles, and we trust that you will use what you like and ignore what is inconsistent with your own style. We think that an instructor's individual style is a very important component of what the students experience. If your are already a successful classroom instructor, you might have a style different from ours that works perfectly well. Even so, you might be able to blend some of our suggestions in with your own methods.

Beyond advocacy, we have adopted an unusual approach in this instructor's manual. Sometimes we are saying things to first-time instructors; other times we are supplying rhetoric you can deliver students if you feel a need to explain why you are teaching the course the way you do. We don't label our paragraphs according to who it's for. Just use what you want.

Oh yes, and we write to you—and many of you are career academics like us—in the second person. Would one prefer a consistent formal adherence to the third person?

About the Solutions

All programs in Parts Four (Output) of the sample executions were run and the output electronically inserted into the text of the Instructor's Manual. All solutions to Parts Five (Programming) were run to ensure correctness.

CONTENTS

COMPUTERS AND PROGRAMMING 1

Chapter 1 is designed so that an instructor can teach it in class or simply assign it on a read-only basis. Some instructors like to give students some explicit background about computers before they start teaching them how to write programs. Others don't want to spend class time on it.

A few students start out wanting to spend a lot of time learning quotable facts about computers before they begin writing and running programs. Some instructors think that such preliminaries can be motivational, and they are for some students. For the most part, we think that learning about computers before using them is too much like learning quotable facts about reading or writing before you do any.

This chapter provides a comprehensive overview of what the process of writing computer programs will be like. It introduces many of the important computer science buzzwords and terminology. The sections of this chapter are germain to the main purposes of the course: teaching problem-solving skills, top-down program design, Fortran syntax and programming, and debugging. They should be read, but not too closely, because, unlike the rest of the book, the student is not being asked to reproduce and extend the examples in this chapter.

Don't get trapped in overly long discussions of whether device X has attribute Y. The classification of automatic devices, like the classification of biological species, is based on perceived similarities. While most mammals don't lay eggs, some marsupials do, and are still considered mammals. So let it be with computers. The fact that device X doesn't have property Y doesn't "prove" it isn't a computer.

Sections 1.2 and 1.3 on top-down design are of value both to rank beginners and to students experienced in other computer programming languages, but not in the structured programming style. Section 1.2 treats the problem-solving methodology in general terms; Section 1.3 treats them in specific terms. Tell your students not to expect to write a Fortran program like PAYROL this early in the semester. The fact that they can almost read such a Fortran program is an indication of the degree of naturalness of the language.

The point of talking about the history of Fortran and computer programming is to emphasize the relative recentness of the entire discipline and the relative antiquity within the discipline of the language Fortran.

The challenge of teaching Chapter 1 is balancing the benefits to the student of knowing a little about what a computer is and how it is programmed against the drawback of delaying the writing of the student's first program.

Getting Started

The purpose of Chapter 1 is to get students oriented to the capabilities of computers and to the discipline of computer programming. Many students feel more comfortable if they think they know something about computers before they try to write their first computer program.

One way to teach the early part of this chapter might be called the "Babbage-almost-got-it-right" method. You can describe what Babbage's Analytic Engine could have done if it had actually been built and say how little a modern computer differs from it for most of the ten attributes. Additional information is given by Morrison and Morrison in Charles Babbage and His Calculating Engines, Dover 1961.

Another way to present this material is the "hand-calculator-as-an-introduction-to-computers" method. Especially for the attributes of arithmetic, memory, input, output, and programmability, this approach works well.

Pitfalls

Pitfall 1: overemphasis on the taxonomy of automatic devices. Although categorization is a worthy pursuit, the emphasis should be to describe the ten attributes as properties of he computers your students will be using. It doesn't matter much whether something lacking Attribute 9 can still be called a computer. A better question (whose answer lies far beyond what a beginner could grasp in the first week of the semester) is what kinds of programs couldn't be executed on a device that lacks such and such an attribute.

Pitfall 2: explaining hardware before the students have experience writing programs. What a beginning student needs to know about hardware is that it is something that executes programs. A few informational gems sprinkled here and there can be entertaining, but what matters is that computers can execute Fortran programs. You don't need lectures on nutrition and digestion to get started eating, and you don't need lectures on hardware to get started programming.

No Examination Questions on Chapter 1

We recommend giving no exam questions on Chapter 1. We don't expect students to capture the spirit of the course from this chapter. It is atypical.

Vocabulary

address, of a memory cell
algorithm
alternative computational procedures
assignment operator
assignment statement
automatic operation
bottom-up program testing
bug
call a subprogram
calling program
compiler
computer
computer program
computer terminal
data transfer
debugging
decision
divide and conquer
documentation
hard copy
indirect addressing
initialization
input
input buffer
loop
machine language
magnetic disk
magnetic tape
main program
memory
memory cell
module
output
output buffer
program memory, in a calculator
programmable
pseudocode
punchcard
sorting
subprogram
successive refinement
top-down design of programs
top-down program testing
variable name

Chapter Outline

PROGRAM SOLVING AND PROGRAMMING IN FORTRAN 2

For most persons new to computer programming, the biggest hurdle is writing and running a first program. We try to get students over that hurdle as soon as possible, usually by the end of the first week. There is nothing quite like the warm glow and realization of "I can do it!" that accompanies this initial success. Obviously, the act of writing a program precedes the act of getting it to run on a computer, but it doesn't follow that students ought to learn writing programs first and running them second.

Teaching running first and writing second is a conservative strategy for getting students past that big hurdle. Even before you start teaching how to write programs, you can give the students the assignment of getting one of the easy programs in the text to run. It helps enormously if your facilities and Fortran system are user friendly so that every student can be required to do this assignment unassisted—or almost unassisted.

This won't be an easy assignment for students with no previous computer experience. They won't be familiar with the differences between a computer keyboard and a typewriter keyboard. They won't know anything about line editors, much less about screen editors. They won't even know, at first, whether they are communicating with the editor or the operating system. They are going to experience cultural shock.

As you may have gathered, Chapter 1 doesn't fit perfectly into our chapter-a-week plan. If many of your students are true beginners at programming, then you will need the time you saved on Chapter 1 to help your students master Chapter 2. There isn't a lot of Fortran syntax introduced in Chapter 2, but the amount of new syntax to be learned is only one of the variables that affect the time and effort it takes students to master a chapter.

There couldn't be anything more important pedagogically than getting your students to leave the context of asking you what works and entering the context of running programs themselves on a computer. If you can do that, then in a limited way you will have turned them into independent thinkers; they will be their own experts.

Prepare Step-By-Step Instructions for Using the Computer

To guide them past this "sink-or-swim" encounter, prepare an absolutely complete step-by-step set of instructions telling your students how to run the program CALC1 on the computer system that is available to them. Make sure it explains what to do after a typing mistake. You should not include every last detail of screen editing, just one or two of the simplest all-purpose editing commands, such as erasing a character in the current line or retyping a line. Additional capabilities of your editor can be introduced as the semester progresses.

If you are lucky, you have a highly capable teaching assistant who can write these instructions for you. It ought to run one or two pages long. Students need a copy of these instructions the first time they go to the computer.

Every Student Needs an Immediate Personal Success Experience

Is it okay for you or a teaching assistant to help students get a first program running? Of course it is—that's why we say "almost unassisted". However, a student who gets the slightest trace of help in running a first program ought to repeat the steps entirely without aid from anyone. Watching is not the same as doing. If your students work in groups, tell them that each of them is to go through the same steps to get the program running. Otherwise, the watchers won't learn even a small fraction as much as the doers.

Which Comes First, Syntax or Examples?

Now let's talk about writing programs. A well-written Fortran program often "makes sense" to English-speaking persons who don't know the Fortran language. Many Fortran statements look a great deal like slightly stilted English sentences tempered with traces of mathematical usage.

There is a very important difference between a natural language environment (i.e., English, French, Chinese) and a computer-language environment. Although experienced speakers of a natural language can often understand amazingly diverse approximations to correct language usage, a Fortran compiler or interpreter is quite unforgiving of even minor grammatical transgressions.

On the other hand, people are usually more adept at learning new languages (and other things) by generalizing from examples and successful experiences than at learning them from syntax descriptions or sets of rules. Certainly no one gives an infant grammar lessons.

So what do you present the students first, examples or syntax? In the classroom, we like to start with an example or two, and then mix them both in together, just as we have done in the text.

What Good Are Computers? None Without Output!

One of the less amusing features of some of the old style programming manuals was that they began by explaining how to do calculations, and deferred discussion of output for a long time.

Thus, the reader was expected to wade through pages of ill timed details of calculations before seeing how to get any useful work out of a computer. To be sure, there were some justifications then for postponing discussion of output, and there are some today, but in the balance, they don't make sense for beginning students.

If computers didn't produce output, they wouldn't be any good at all. The brightest and slowest of students all want to know what good are computers.

Only the apathetic and the docile students don't want to know what good they are before investing a lot of effort in learning how to program them.

Lively students want to know what good computers will do for them personally very soon. So we teach them right away how to get output. Seeing is believing.

Variable Input Is What Ultimately Saves Human Effort

If a person can do accurate arithmetic and type neatly, there would scarcely be a reason to write a program for a fixed calculation. After all, it's probably easer to do the steps of the calculation on a hand calculator than to write them out in a computer language.

When you have to apply the same calculation to more than one set of numbers or other data, there is a good chance that writing the instructions once and having them reapplied with automatic perfection every subsequent time you need them will ultimately yield a savings in total effort and cost.

Interactive vs. Batch Input

Some Fortran systems have interactive program execution; some do not. In this book, we apply the term "batch execution" to all noninteractive execution. It does not matter whether several jobs in the same computer language are collected and compiled together or not. The diagnostic criterion we use is whether the input data for the execution is prepared in advance and placed in advance in a computer readable file. If the input data is in a pre-prepared file, then we call the execution "batch", even if the computer is a stand alone microcomputer with only one user. If the input data are keyed in during execution, then the execution is interactive. This distinction makes good sense from the programmer's and user's point of view.

Which kind of execution should we use? If only one kind is available, then use it. Most programs can be written for either mode, with only minor modifications in the input sequences of instructions.

Given a choice, we prefer interactive execution if the amount of input data is small and batch execution if it is large. There is no substitute for the immediacy and thrill of interactive execution. You type your data and immediately get your answers.

The problems arise when the amount of data is large. Programs rarely work perfectly the first time. (The small programs of this section do, if they are typed very carefully, but that is an exception.) When you are debugging a program interactively, you often wind up entering all the data (when prompted) and then the program fails. You make a change, recompile, execute, and retype all the data. The program again fails, perhaps in a different way if your correction had any effect. You make another change, recompile, execute, and again retype all the data.

Batch input files do not disappear after an execution, successful or not. If the execution was unsuccessful and a correction is attempted, the input file does not have to be retyped for the next execution, nor for the one after.

We prefer batch input files in these circumstances because we hate to redo the same work. There is a fundamental principle of efficient computer usage that the same value should not have to be entered twice (unless the repetition is for purposes of error detection and correction).

Some applications such as computer-assisted instruction make no sense for batch execution, and some applications have so much data that interactive input is out of the question. We do some of each.

Echoes and Prompts

It is never too early to learn good programming habits. Batch input should be echoed to the standard output device. There are so many reasons why this should be done and so few circumstances where it is impossible that it is not unreasonable to insist that all student projects echo their input data.

We wish to emphasize two benefits of echoes of input data. First, the practical benefit that the grader can see what input data was used to calculate the printed answers. Second, the usefulness of echoes of input data in debugging.

There is many a slip between the intention to put a value in an input file and the successful reading of that value into the correct variable in a Fortran program. The value could be wrong in the first place. It could be mistyped in the file. It could be in the wrong column (which is why you should avoid formatted input) or interchanged with another value. The format could be wrong or the types of the input value and the variable in the READ list incompatible. The READ list could be in the wrong order. An echo of input data tells you whether one of these things went wrong, or whether the bug must be sought in some other part of the program.

Since in its final state, a computer program has no bugs, verification of correct execution is as important as detection of incorrect execution. Echoes of input data play an important role.

Interactive input provides an opportunity for a display of user friendliness or user unfriendliness. An input prompt tells the user exactly what input is expected in response to the next READ statement. Input prompts can be very informative, somewhat informative, cryptic, or even absent. Which would you prefer, a prompt requesting you to type your name, first name first and last name last, or one requesting you to type your name with no indication of order, or a simple uninformative question mark, or nothing—the program just stops waiting for input of some unspecified kind? Insist that your students give you informative input prompts.

The Man-Machine Interface

People have to supply data for use in computer programs, and people have to read the output of the computer programs. Sometimes the form that the user finds most natural for representing the data is also the form most easily used in the calculations. That makes the programmer's life very easy. Sometimes they are not the same. In that case, the question of friendliness or unfriendliness for the user of a program depends on who must do the work of meeting the other's preferences.

If the user must talk to the computer using the computer's internal formats and read an awkward and disorganized printout, the program is unpleasant to use. If the computer does the translations and the user uses natural (for humans) representations of the data, the program is friendly.

A Dialogue about Uninformative Variable Names

Consider the following scenario. A student comes to a computer programming clinician to get help debugging a program with uninformative variable names.

Clinician: What do the values of this variable X represent?

Student (annoyed at being asked so obvious a question): Oh, they are the count of the number of blanks in the input string. Anyone can see that.

Clinician: Then why don't you call it NRBLNK?

Student (shrugs)

Clinician: Where is X incremented?

Student: Right here in the main input loop.

Clinician: It seems to be in the wrong branch of the test IF (C .EQ. ' ')
THEN

Student: You're right.

Clinician (moralizing): You probably wouldn't have make that mistake if
you had called it NRBLNK instead of X. By the way, what is Y?

Student: It's the number of nonblanks.

Clinician: Then why do you increment it in both branches of the IF test for
blanks?

Student: Well, maybe it's the total number of characters. I'm not sure.

.
.
.

Need we say more?

Formatted Output

We teach formatted output in Fortran so early because many Fortran systems
we have used print all real values by default in E format, even values that are
not extremely large or small. E format on most systems is not even standard
"scientific notation". Only people forced to look at it for years become truly
comfortable with it. Format specifiers of the form 1PEn.d give one digit to the
left of the decimal point in the mantissa as in standard scientific notation.

When we have bad defaults on our student system, we teach output format-
ting very early. When we have good default output formats, as we did on the
system used for the sample executions, we can delay it a while. There is no
denying that beautiful output is easier to read. Fortran makes producing beautiful output very easy. Why settle for less?

Roundoff

If you are lucky, you won't have to explain roundoff in Chapter 2. If you are
unlucky, every one of your student's calculations with reals will show roundoff
in the printed output, and they will all be clambering for an explanation, and in
danger of losing the faith that the computer is very good and very accurate at
arithmetic.

We have two machines side by side. One almost never shows roundoff,
even on the worst numerical dirty tricks we plan for it. The other falls into
every roundoff trap under the sun.

If you must explain roundoff, the concept that the best representation of
$1/3$ is 0.333333 and that $3 * (1/3)$ calculates as $3 * 0.333333 = 0.999999$ and
not as 1.00000 is relatively easy to grasp.

Style Notes

Important elements of good programming style are set off in highlighted
displays. While it is too much to hope for your personal programming style to
agree in all particulars with ours, the important point to emphasize to your students is that the goal is to write readable programs.

We do not claim to have a corner on the market of good programming style. We ask (perhaps insist is more nearly correct) that our students try it our way to start. Thereafter, we are open to discussion as to whether our programming style served the goal of writing readable programs. We ask you as a fellow professional to consider our programming style, to accept and transmit to your students those elements of our style you agree with, and to replace those elements you reject with your own ideas. The discussion of the goals of good programming style may be more important than the actual style aimed for.

Case Studies

Every chapter has at least one case study section. (Some chapters have more, and some additional case studies are not complete sections.) A case study is a portion of the book where the application is the primary focus, along with the techniques of programming that application in Fortran.

Each case study is a real world problem, presented and solved in the order that things are done in the real world. First, there is background information setting the context for the problem. Then there is a statement of the problem. Next there is a discussion of facts, formulas, and techniques that might be of use in the solution. Then there is an initial attempt at the solution, usually in pseudocode. Then the pseudocode is systematically refined to an executable Fortran program. Finally, the program is tested and the sample output discussed.

The case study in this chapter is the first of three dealing with the quadratic formula. Most students will be familiar with this formula from high school algebra. The point of using the quadratic formula in this chapter is that it is a complicated mathematical formula to program in Fortran.

Program Testing

It is never too early to learn good program testing habits. Many programs work for the most typical test cases, but fail for extreme or atypical input data values. The program QUAD is no exception.

We test QUAD first with progressively "harder" typical cases yielding two distinct roots. The first has integral roots and is easily checked. The second has rational roots, and the third has irrational roots. Next we test the limiting case of a quadratic equation with a double root, and it still works. Finally, we test the program QUAD on a quadratic formula that has no real roots. Not surprisingly, it fails. We didn't really expect it to work. There is no way to store a complex value for a root in a variable declared type real.

Every program has limitations. There is nothing to be done about this limitation until some more Fortran syntax is taught. The user will have to be told, "Don't use the program QUAD to solve quadratic equations with complex roots." This puts a burden on the user, but it is the best we can do in Chapter 2. What we are setting up is the two additional case studies on the quadratic formula. When we teach IF statements, we can distinguish between the cases of real vs. complex roots by calculating and testing the discriminant, the expression under the square root. Complex roots can then be handled by a different sequence of steps, culminating in printing the real and imaginary parts of the roots. The third time we come back to the quadratic formula, we introduce the data type COMPLEX.

Testing and Debugging

Every chapter that introduces new syntactic material has a section on testing and debugging. The format is much like a case study with background information, the problem statement, and the steps leading to the solution. However in the Testing and Debugging Sections, the Fortran program written to solve the problem is wrong!

The intent in the Testing and Debugging sections is to simulate as nearly as possible the real world environment a programmer faces when a first attempt at writing a program doesn't work. Some programs contain more than one bug. Some bugs only become visible when other bugs are fixed.

Since few programs of any size work properly the first time they are run, it is as important to the student to develop good debugging skills as it is to develop good programming skills. One prevents many of the errors from happening, and the other catches and corrects the remaining errors.

Detecting and correcting syntax errors is only the first step in debugging. In some sense, it is the most trivial step. (The sense is that it is easily automated, as most compilers do a pretty good job of detecting, but not correcting, syntax errors.) The real meat of testing and debugging is locating and correcting algorithmic errors. Of course, it doesn't hurt to become familiar with the traps and pitfalls of the Fortran language if you want your programs to run.

Vocabulary

assignment statement
batch execution
bug
built-in function
character constant
character data type
character string
comment
compiler
debugging
default format
default type for a variable
echo of input data
exponential notation
format
format descriptor
format specification
input prompt
integer data type
interactive editing of programs and data
interactive execution
interactive input
interpreter
keyword
linker
number
operating system
parameter
parameter assignment
positional notation
program
program name
program listing
real data type
roundoff error
running a program
scheduling algorithm
signed number
statement label
time sharing
type
type declaration
user friendly
variable

Chapter Outline

Examination Questions

Part One: True or False

Indicate which of the sentences below are true, and which are false. If a sentence is false, explain what is wrong.

1. Addition, subtraction, multiplication, and division are valid operations in Fortran, but raising to a power is not allowed because computer input devices cannot type the power above the line as a superscript.

2. The default PRINT format is specified by an asterisk (*).

3. Fortran is a scientific computer programming language and can only process numeric data types.

4. Input data is echoed to an output device to verify that it was read correctly.

5. Character string variables have a fixed length in Fortran.

Part Two: Fill In

Complete the sentences below to make them true.

1. The major difference between a variable and a parameter is _____.

2. Fortran statements are typed in columns _____.

3. In the Fortran expression A + B * C ** D, the operation that is performed first is _____.

4. Exponential notation is preferred over positional notation for _____ numbers.

5. A Fortran statement is continued to a second line by _____.

6. The value of the expression 1/2 is _____.

Part Three: Syntax

Indicate which of the Fortran programs or sequences of statements are syntactically correct, and which are not. If a program or statement is not correct, rewrite it to make it correct, or indicate why this is not possible. Be sure not to change the "intent" of the statement in the process of correcting the syntax.

1.
```
PROGRAM EX2.1
PRINT 37.2 * 45
END
```

2.
```
PROGRAM EX2
PRINT *, 'HELLO'
END
```

3.
```
PROGRAM EXAMPLE3
PRINT '(3F10.5)', 5.0, 6.7, 8.8/9.9
```

4.
```
PROGRAM
INTEGER X, Y, Z
X = 5
READ Y, Z
PRINT X * Y * Z
END
```

5.

```
PROGRAM FIVE
REAL A, B, C, D, SUM
PARAMETER (X = 1.2, Y = 3.4,
           Z = 4.5, W = 6.7)
SUM = A + B + C + D
PRINT *, 'A + B + C + D = ', SUM
END
```

Part Four: Output

What output will be printed when the following programs are run? If the output is formatted, use b's to indicate clearly the blank columns in the output.

1.

```
PROGRAM ONE
PRINT *, 3 * 5
END
```

2.

```
PROGRAM TWO
PRINT *, (5.7 + 6.23) / 2
END
```

3.

```
PROGRAM THREE
REAL A, B
READ *, A, B, C
PRINT *, 'INPUT VALUES:  ', A, B, C
PRINT '(A, F5.2)', 'AVERAGE:', (A + B + C) / 3
END
```

The input file contains the following line.

1.2 2.3 4.5

4.

```
PROGRAM FOUR
PRINT *, (1 + 2.0/ 3.0 * 4.0 ** 2) / 6 * 7
END
```

Part Five: Programming

Write complete Fortran programs to solve the following problems.

1. The Problem: A light year is the distance that light travels in one year. Calculate the length of one light year in meters. Print the answer with an identifying message. Background Information: Light travels at the rate of 3×10 meters/sec. Assume that there are 365.25 days in an average year.

2. The Problem: In a shot put competition, the longest of a contestant's three tosses is the only distance that is counted. Write a program that reads three distances and prints the longest. Echo all input data, and identify the answer as the longest. Hint: Use the built-in function MAX. Input Data: One line with three distances.

30.5 49.6 44.5

Sample Output:

```
RUN SHOT
INPUT DATA  DISTANCES:  30.5 49.6 44.5
THE LONGEST IS 49.6
```

Answer Key

Part One: True or False

1. False, raising to a power is denoted by **.
2. True.
3. False. Character strings are supported.
4. True.
5. True.

Part Two: Fill In

1. a parameter cannot change during an execution.
2. 7-72
3. raising to a power, C ** D.
4. very large and very small numbers.
5. typing a character other than blank or zero in column 6 of each continuation line.
6. 0 (The quotient of two integer constants gives an integer answer.)

Part Three: Syntax

1.
```
        PROGRAM EX21                    <--program name
        PRINT *, 37.2 * 45              <--default format
        END
```

2.
```
        PROGRAM EX2                     <--no changes in this program
        PRINT *, 'HELLO'
        END
```

3.
```
        PROGRAM EX3                     <--name too long
        PRINT '(3F10.5)', 5.0, 6.7, 8.8/9.9
        END                             <--missing END
```

4.
```
        PROGRAM NONAME                  <--missing name
        INTEGER X, Y, Z
        X = 5
        READ *, Y, Z                    <--missing format
        PRINT *, X * Y * Z              <--missing format
        END
```

5.
```
        PROGRAM FIVE
        REAL A, B, C, D, SUM
        PARAMETER (A = 1.2, B = 3.4,    <--parameter names (see note)
     +          C = 4.5, D = 6.7)       <--missing continuation in col 6
        SUM = A + B + C + D
        PRINT *, 'A + B + C + D = ', SUM
        END
```

Although the use of parameters X, Y, Z, and W is not a syntax error (they have default type real), execution will terminate on an undefined variable error in the calculation of SUM is the names are not changed.

Part Four: Output

1.
RUN ONE
 15
2.
RUN TWO
 5.96500

(Equivalent E format answers are also acceptable)

3.
RUN THREE
INPUT VALUES: 1.20000 2.30000 4.50000
AVERAGE:b2.67

4.
 13.6111

Part Five: Programming

1.
```
      PROGRAM LTYEAR
C     CALCULATE AND PRINT THE NUMBER OF METERS IN A LIGHT YEAR
      DIST = 3.E8 * 60 * 60 * 24 * 365.25
      PRINT *, 'A LIGHT YEAR IS ', DIST, ' METERS'
      END
```

RUN LTYEAR
A LIGHT YEAR IS 0.946728E+15 METERS

2.
```
      PROGRAM SHOT
C     READS THREE DISTANCES AND PRINTS THE LARGEST
      READ *, D1, D2, D3
      PRINT *, 'INPUT DATA  DISTANCES:  ', D1, D2, D3
      PRINT *, 'THE LONGEST IS ', MAX (D1, D2, D3)
      END
```

RUN SHOT
INPUT DATA DISTANCES: 30.5 49.6 44.5
THE LONGEST IS 49.6

DECISION STRUCTURES 3

Chapter 3 explains how to program the computer so that it decides between alternative actions at execution time. Of course, the capacity to make decisions is the basis for seemingly intelligent behavior.

IF Blocks

For many students, the program ESCAPE is where the course begins to be self-motivating. Once you show the students how to program a decision between a rocket reaching a maximum altitude and returning to Earth and a rocket escaping from the Earth's gravitational field, they can see a wealth of possibilities.

The IF block allows the computer to react flexibly and adaptively to the input data. If you see a computer blindly reacting in the same way whether it is appropriate or inappropriate for the situation at hand, it is because some computer programmer did not take the trouble to distinguish between the cases and provide different executable code for each essentially different case.

Comparison With Other Computer Programming Languages

If your students know other programming languages, you can point out the difference between the Fortran IF block and the IF statement in other languages. The Fortran IF block allows more than one statement in each alternative, a situation that happens most of the time, without the excess baggage of begin-end blocks (compound statements).

While the single-statement THEN clause and ELSE clause of languages such as Pascal, ALGOL, and PL/I please the theoretician because they provide an elegant means of allowing more variety in the language than first meets the eye, they are an equal nuisance to the practical writer of computer programs for precisely the same reason. The most common programming error in these languages is mismatched begin and end statements, exceeded only by the trivial error of omitted semicolons.

The Fortran IF block also allows any number of alternatives with ELSE IF clauses. Many other languages have only a two-alternative IF statement.

Programming Style

When we discuss the relative merits of mutually exclusive IF tests vs. nonexclusive IF tests, the purpose is not so much to settle the issue as to raise the question and to discuss the criteria for deciding it. Even beginning programmers should know that the goals are readability, provable correctness, ease of debugging, and ease of modification.

Students with some programming experience, but in an undisciplined style, are the hardest to convince that programming style is worth talking about. After all, their programs run without it. Even with these students, you are sowing seeds of good programming practice which may some day bloom when these students finally get tired of making the same avoidable mistakes.

Flowcharts

Ordinarily, we do not use flowcharts for program planning. The top-down methodology and successive refinements in pseudocode provide a more reliable tool. However, flowcharts are unsurpassed for illustrating the flow of control in IF blocks and nested IF blocks.

What is wrong with flowcharts for program planning? The simplest answer is that flowcharting permits arrows to be drawn from any box to any other box. When coded into a computer language, this is equivalent to the unrestricted use of GO TO statements. The code that results from a flowchart is often unstructured, difficult to debug, modify, and maintain.

Post hoc, to illustrate how a structured program works, flowcharts are wonderful. We use them all the time.

One problem with flowcharts is the lack of an adequate and standardized representation of the DO statement, the primary loop control statement. The DO statement of most programming languages is at a higher level than the flowchart boxes that refine it. There are several partially successful attempts to flowchart a DO loop. Use your favorite.

Older Fortran IF statements

Fortran 77 still supports two older IF statements, the logical IF and the arithmetic IF. There are few constructs in programming with the potential for confusion of the arithmetic IF statement. The authors, having used it when there was no other, eagerly welcomed its successor. Successful use of the arithmetic IF is a virtuoso skill. One laments that the world no longer needs such virtuoso skills, while at the same time one rejoices that it is no longer necessary to keep one's own virtuoso skill up to performance levels.

We believe that, in the beginning, one good way to do something is sufficient. (Notice, we say one "good" way; one bad way is not sufficient.) The logical IF statement allows exactly the same kinds of flexible IF tests as the IF block, and in certain circumstances it is even a few lines shorter.

However, the full IF block is the bread and butter of structured programming of alternatives. We must teach our students the full IF block. The question we asked ourselves is "for the first go round, is it worth writing a few extra END IFs to avoid teaching another construct?" Our answer was yes. There is little inconvenience, and students can learn the logical IF later. As always, we feel the discussion is more important than the answer.

Quadratic Equations

The background of your students may determine the extent you wish to emphasize the quadratic equation case study. Assuming that students understand the problem, it has a lot to say about program design and testing. For students with strong mathematical background, the complex data type of Fortran is a feature found in few other languages. It is one of the reasons why Fortran is widely used in science and engineering.

Character Strings

Number crunching is only one part of computing. Character data is equally important, and should not be neglected. The facility for comparing character strings will ultimately lead to sorting and searching lists of character strings. Meanwhile, simple character variables and constants help make the answers understandable.

Comparing Fortran character strings to those in other languages, we see some good features and some bad. It does not have variable length character strings like BASIC, but at least assignments and comparisons can be made between character strings of different lengths, unlike standard Pascal. (This is the reason why Pascal has so many mutually incompatible nonstandard extensions for character strings.)

Testing and Debugging

Every new programming feature requires a new way (or ways) of testing the programs that use it. For IF blocks, the most important point is that test cases should be designed to exercise every alternative in the IF block.

Random test cases or whatever comes to mind in the way of data is not enough. A hundred random cases can still leave sections of code untested. The programmer knows best what cases the computer is programmed to distinguish, and so the programmer knows best how to manufacture test data to test whether the program correctly recognizes the cases and does the right thing in each case.

Another point of potential trouble is the boundary lines between cases. In the quadratic formula programs, a discriminant (the quantity under the square root) of zero is the boundary between cases where the square root can be successfully extracted resulting in two real roots, and cases where attempting to extract the square root of a negative number will cause and error termination of the program.

With reals, roundoff may enter the picture, and the boundary point may never be exactly reached. With integers, it is usually reached exactly, and its being handled the wrong way is a common error. These cases should be tested also.

When your students write a programming assignment with an IF block, do not settle for only one sample execution. The sample executions a student submits should prove that the program handles *all* the cases.

Vocabulary

ASCII character set
character set
collating sequence
complex data type
EBCDIC character set
ELSE IF statement
ELSE statement
END IF statement
IF block
IF statement
IF test
inverse built-in functions CHAR and ICHAR
logical data type
logical expression
logical operators .AND., .OR., and .NOT.
mutually exclusive conditions in an IF block
nested IF blocks
nonexclusive conditions in an IF block

Chapter Outline

Examination Questions

Part One: True or False

Indicate which of the sentences below are true, and which are false. If a sentence is false, explain what is wrong.

1. An IF block starts with the keyword IF and ends with the keyword END IF.

2. The ELSE clause is optional in an IF block.

3. If the condition in an IF test is true, then the following Fortran statement is executed; otherwise the statement after is executed.

4. The maximum depth to which IF blocks can be nested in Fortran is seven.

5. In a correctly formed IF block, exactly one of the IF or ELSE IF conditions is true during each execution of the block.

Part Two: Multiple Choice

Choose the one best answer.

1. Which of the following parts of an IF block may not be omitted?
    a. the IF test
    b. the ELSE IF tests
    c. the ELSE statement
    d. the END IF statement

2. Which of the following are arithmetic comparison operators in Fortran?
    a. <, >, and =
    b. .LT., .GT., and =
    c. .AND., .OR., and .NOT.
    d. .LT., .GT., and .NE.
    e. LT, GT, and EQ

3. IF blocks are used
    a. to handle different cases by different sequences of Fortran statements.
    b. to prevent program termination in case of input data that cannot be handled.
    c. to shorten a Fortran program.
    d. all of the above.
    e. a and b above.

4. The shortest possible meaningful IF block is
    a. 1 line long.
    b. 2 lines long.
    c. 3 lines long.
    d. 4 lines long.
    e. 5 lines long.

5. One IF block may be nested within
    a. the THEN clause of another IF block.
    b. the ELSE clause of another IF block.
    c. an ELSE IF clause of another IF block.
    d. all of the above.
    e. a and c above, but not b.

6. The condition in an IF or ELSE IF test must be

  a.   true.
  b.   an arithmetic expression.
  c.   the result of comparing two arithmetic expressions.
  d.   a logical variable.
  e.   a logical expression.

7.   Character string comparisons

  a.   depend only on the first letters of the character strings.
  b.   are an extension of alphabetic order.
  c.   are prohibited between strings of different lengths.
  d.   take meaning into account.
  e.   may not be used in an IF test or ELSE IF test.

8.   The built-in function ICHAR

  a.   returns an integer value.
  b.   is the inverse of the built-in function CHAR.
  c.   has a value which depends on the character set used by the computer.
  d.   returns a smaller value for characters earlier in the collating sequence.
  e.   all of the above.

9.   Proper testing of an IF block requires

  a.   randomly chosen data.
  b.   "real" data not contrived by the programmer.
  c.   test cases designed to test all alternatives in the IF block.
  d.   test cases designed to test the breakpoints between cases. e. c, d, and
       b above in that order of importance.

10. In the absence of parentheses, which of the following operators has the
     highest precedence, that is, which is performed first?

  a.   +
  b.   *
  c.   .AND.
  d.   .OR.
  e.   .LT.

Part Three: Syntax

Indicate which of the following Fortran programs or sequence of statements are
syntactically correct, and which are not. If a program or statement is not correct, rewrite it to make it correct, or indicate why this is not possible. Be sure
not to change the "intent" of the statement in the process of correcting the syntax. Assume all variables are correctly declared.

1.
```
IF A .LT. B THEN
   Z = 1
ELSE
   Z = 2
```

2.
```
IF ((A = B) .AND. (B = C)) THEN
   A = C
ELSE
   A .NE. C
END IF
```

3.
```
IF (A .GT. B) THEN
   LARGER = A
```

```
   ELSE IF (A .EQ. B) THEN
      LARGER = A
   ELSE
      LARGER = B
   END IF
```

4.

```
   IF (A .GT. B) THEN
      LARGER = A
   ELSE
      IF (A .EQ. B) THEN
         LARGER = A
      ELSE
         LARGER = B
   END IF
```

5.

```
   IF (A .GE. B) THEN
      LARGER = A
   END IF
   ELSE
      LARGER = B
   END IF
```

Part Four: Output

What output will be printed when the following programs are run? If the output is formatted, use *b*'s to clearly indicate the blank columns in the output.

1.

```
   PROGRAM ONE
   INTEGER A, B, C
   READ *, A, B, C
   PRINT *, A, B, C
   IF (A .GT. B) THEN
      PRINT *, A, ' IS LARGER'
   ELSE
      PRINT *, B, ' OR ', C IS LARGER.
   END IF
   END
```

The input file contains the values

12 23 34

2.

```
   PROGRAM TWO
   INTEGER X, Y, Z
   X = 4
   Y = 3
   Z = X + Y
   IF (X .GT. Y) THEN
      X = Y
      Z = X + Y
   ELSE
      Z = 5
   END IF
   Z = Z * 2
```

```
IF (Z .GT. 8) THEN
    PRINT *, Z, ' IS LARGE'
ELSE
    PRINT *, Z, ' IS SMALL'
END IF
END
```

Part Five: Programming

Write complete Fortran programs to solve the following problems.

1. The Problem: The alphabet, 'ABCDEFGHIJKLMNOPQRSTUVWXYZ',
    is a sequence of 26 letters which may be considered circular by adhering to
    the convention that the letter immediately following 'Z' is 'A'. This con-
    vention allows the end of the alphabet to "wrap around" to the beginning
    of the alphabet. The program should read as input a letter of the alphabet
    (uppercase only) and a number N. The answer should be the letter of the
    alphabet that is N letters later in the alphabet than the input letter. If the
    value of N is negative, the answer should be N letters before the input
    letter. In both directions, the sequence of letters should wrap around from
    one end of the alphabet to the other. Sample Input:

'C'	5	H
'Z'	1	A
'A'	-1	Z
'X'	6	D

Answer Key

Part One: True or False

1. True.

2. True.

3. False, all statements between the IF test and the next ELSE IF or ELSE statement are executed.

4. False, such limits are implementation specific.

5. False, there are examples to the contrary in the text.

Part Two: Multiple Choice

1. a, the IF test.

2. d, the other choices all contain mistakes.

3. e, IF blocks don't primarily shorten programs.

4. c, the IF test, the THEN clause, and the END IF statement.

5. d, all of the above.

6. e, a logical expression.

7. b, extend alphabetic order.

8. e, all of the above.

9. e, this is the best answer.

10. b, all arithmetic operators precede all comparison operators, which precede all logical operators.

Part Three: Syntax

1.

```
      IF (A .LT. B) THEN            <--missing parentheses
         Z = 1
      ELSE
         Z = 2
      END IF                        <--missing
```

2.

```
      IF ((A .EQ. B) .AND. (B .EQ. C)) THEN  <--wrong comparison oper.
         A = C
      ELSE
         A = C                      <--assignment operator is =
      END IF
```

3.

```
      IF (A .GT. B) THEN            <--correct IF block
         LARGER = A
      ELSE IF (A .EQ. B) THEN
         LARGER = A
      ELSE
         LARGER = B
      END IF
```

4.

```
      IF (A .GT. B) THEN
         LARGER = A
      ELSE
```

```
      IF (A .EQ. B) THEN
         LARGER = A
      ELSE
         LARGER = B
      END IF                        <--missing END IF
   END IF
```

5.
```
   IF (A .GE. B) THEN
      LARGER = A
                                    <--extra END IF deleted
   ELSE
      LARGER = B
   END IF
```

Part Four: Output

1.
```
RUN ONE
     12    23    34
     23 OR    34 IS LARGER
```

2.
```
RUN TWO
     12 IS LARGE
```

Part Five: Programming

1.
```
      PROGRAM WRAP
C     READS A LETTER L AND A NUMBER N
C     PRINTS THE LETTER N POSITIONS AFTER L
C     ALPHABET WRAP AND NEGATIVE RELATIVE POSITIONS ARE SUPPORTED
      CHARACTER L *1, ANSWER *1
      INTEGER N, ANSPOS, LPOS
      PRINT *, 'RUN WRAP'
      READ *, L, N
      PRINT *, 'INPUT DATA  LETTER: ', L
      PRINT *, 'INPUT DATA  CHANGE: ', N
      LPOS = ICHAR (L) - ICHAR ('A')
      ANSPOS = MOD (LPOS + N, 26)
      IF (ANSPOS .LT. 0) THEN
         ANSPOS = ANSPOS + 26
      END IF
      ANSWER = CHAR (ICHAR ('A') + ANSPOS)
      PRINT *, 'THE ANSWER IS ', ANSWER
      END

RUN WRAP
INPUT DATA  LETTER: C
INPUT DATA  CHANGE:      5
THE ANSWER IS H
```

```
RUN WRAP
INPUT DATA  LETTER: Z
INPUT DATA  CHANGE:        1
THE ANSWER IS A

RUN WRAP
INPUT DATA  LETTER: A
INPUT DATA  CHANGE:       -1
THE ANSWER IS Z

RUN WRAP
INPUT DATA  LETTER: X
INPUT DATA  CHANGE:        6
THE ANSWER IS D
```

LOOP STRUCTURES 4

The IF block sows the seeds of seemingly intelligent behavior by the computer. The DO delivers on the promise of the computer as a labor saving device. When the student has written a DO block, for the first time the computer can be doing more work in executing the program than the student did in writing it. At this point the student knows that the computer can be useful.

Do not be overly concerned with using efficient algorithms in the beginning. It is more important for the student to realize the enormous power that even the most inefficient algorithms can have when executed at several thousand to several million instructions per second.

Is This the Only Chapter on Loops?

Of course not! Although this is the only chapter with the word "loop" in the title, all the rest of the book is about loops. There is hardly a program in the rest of the book that doesn't use a loop. (Programs to initialize an empty file come to mind as the sole exceptions.)

The power of computer programming is that relatively large goals can be achieved by following relatively simple rules a sufficient number of times. Computers can flawlessly execute repetitive sequences of steps indefinitely, while a human executing the same steps quickly becomes bored, fatigued, and error prone. Thus, algorithms which a human is not likely to carry to a successful completion can be completed successfully with the computer's speed substituting for the lack of sophistication in the algorithm.

Kinds of Loops

Fortran 77 has only one kind of loop block, the DO block. The DO block is ideally suited for certain kinds of computations. If the number of iterations can be predicted before the loop is entered and counted by the DO variable, the DO block is perfect. If the loop requires a sequence of numbers in an arithmetic progression (equal differences), the DO block is perfect.

These are extremely common kinds of loops, but not every loop falls into this pattern. Reading variable length input data, for example, does not. The exact number of items that will be read before termination remains unknown to the program until the moment the termination signal is read. What this application needs is a "DO until exit" loop block with an EXIT statement conditionally executed when the signal is recognized. Fortran doesn't have such a block.

The Fortran programmer or instructor has two choices in this case: (1) abandon the DO block structure and program the input loop as a GO TO loop, or (2) continue to use the DO block for structure, but use a fake number of iterations that is so high that it will never cause termination. In either case, the actual termination (EXIT) is handled by a conditionally executed GO TO statement.

We chose the DO block with early exit alternative on the stylistic principle that we wanted each loop to coded as a loop block. Since Fortran has only one loop block, we find a way to make do with it, bending it to our purposes.

Fake Upper Limits

The fake upper limits on the DO block with exit are not as artificial as they appear at first glance. The computer has only a finite amount of memory and people have only a finite amount of time to wait for the answers from a computer program. A fake upper limit longer than any one of these, or longer than the mean time to a computer hardware error or scheduled shutdown is effectively infinite.

Often a DO block reading variable length data is putting the data into an array. (Not quite yet, but in the next two chapters.) Since an array has the upper and lower limits on its subscripts fixed by its declaration, there is a natural upper bound on the number of data items that can be read. Any more items and there will be no place in the array to store them. In this case, a "DO forever" loop is actually the wrong solution, and a DO block with exit is the correct way to program this application.

Usually there is a natural upper bound on the number of times the body of a loop can possibly be executed before it is clear that something has gone wrong. Most large, multi-user computer systems insist that the user specify a maximum amount of execution time for the job, or they supply a system default. An infinite loop can run up a large computing bill in a short time.

Labels

Programmers accustomed to writing in other computer languages such as Pascal, PL/I, or C are appalled to see statement labels on the final CONTINUE statement of a DO block. The matched keyword pairs conventions in these languages make such labels unnecessary. C uses brackets {} instead of keywords. Perhaps in the next revision of the Fortran standards, DO blocks will end with an END DO statement, and the label will be unnecessary.

The reason Fortran needs a label at the end of a DO block is that a DO block does not have to end with a CONTINUE statement. Most executable Fortran statements that do not alter the normal top to bottom execution sequence can be the last statement in a DO block. For example,

```
      SUM = 0
      DO 18 N = 1, 10
   18 SUM = SUM + N
```

is a valid DO block with preceding initialization. The label 18 is the only way that a Fortran compiler can recognize the end of the DO block.

We do not use any such DO blocks in the book because we believe in the merit of matched keyword pairs. All our DO blocks end with CONTINUE statements.

Private Numbering Conventions

Students reading the book often get the impression that the label on the final CONTINUE statement of a DO block must end in the digit 8. This is of course false—any unsigned integer up to 99999 is acceptable—but it is a harmless misconception. We have adopted this private labelling convention so that the ends of DO blocks are unambiguously flagged by labels that are never used for any other purpose in our programs.

The second part of our private labelling convention is that the next higher label after an end-of-DO block label (ending in the digit 9) is reserved for the early exit from the DO block, if any. Thus, as soon as we begin writing (or later reading) the DO 18 block, we know that the final CONTINUE statement will have label 18 and the early exit will have label 19.

Do-While Loops

Programmers in other computer programming languages have become accustomed to a loop construct called the "Do-while Loop" that has a condition for execution of the next iteration of the loop body placed at the top of the loop. It is sufficiently popular that some dialects of Fortran, such as WATFIV-S, include such a loop structure as a nonstandard extension of Fortran.

Consider, for example, a loop to wait for the first nonzero value in the input file.

```
READ *, VALUE
do-while (VALUE .EQ. 0)
    READ *, VALUE
END do-while
```

Although this loop, or something similar to it, will run under some nonstandard Fortran systems, the do-while statement must be considered as pseudocode when the target language is standard Fortran 77. There is nothing wrong with planning programs using the do-while construct if it is natural to the problem at hand, and we encourage the students to do so. This is especially true if your Fortran system supports do-while. However, we believe that students should be told that do-while is not in the standard, transportable version of Fortran, and that further refinement is necessary to meet that goal.

```
C     FORTRAN 77 REFINEMENT OF A DO WHILE LOOP
      READ *, VALUE
      DO 18 COUNT = 1, LARGE
          IF (VALUE .NE. 0) THEN
              GO TO 19
          END IF
          READ *, VALUE
   18 CONTINUE
   19 ...
```

The chief virtue of the do-while loop, when available, is that labels are not required. A secondary consideration is that with a do-while loop, you do not have to think about real or fake upper bounds on the number of iterations, a mixed blessing.

People programming in computer languages where do-while is available have become very proficient at its use for the same reasons that we have adopted DO blocks with exits, namely that it is there, it works reasonably well, and it is almost the right way to program some applications.

Looking at the do-while construct critically, its chief fault is the necessity of having the exit test at the very top of the loop. As a result, do-while blocks often have a section of code that appears once as an initialization for the loop, and then appears a second time at the bottom of the loop body. In the example above, the statement

```
READ *, VALUE
```

is so repeated.

The DO block with exit is a more powerful construction that does not require this subterfuge. The same READ statement can be used for both the first and all subsequent input values.

```
    DO 18 COUNT = 1, LARGE
        READ *, VALUE
        IF (VALUE .NE. 0) THEN
            GO TO 19
        END IF
 18 CONTINUE
 19 ...
```

If conserving lines of source code is a goal, then the logical IF statement can be used to save two of them.

```
    DO 18 COUNT = 1, LARGE
        READ *, VALUE
            IF (VALUE .NE. 0) GO TO 19
 18 CONTINUE
 19 ...
```

We are aware of the popularity of the do-while construct which we attribute to familiarity with other programming languages where it is the best loop construct for many purposes. We give these explanations to the instructor who is wondering why there aren't more examples of do-while loops in our book. We feel that do-while loops have three major drawbacks for our purposes:

1.   It is not available in standard Fortran 77.
2.   It is a less powerful loop construct than DO block with exit.
3.   It sometimes forces stylistically undesirable duplications of sections of code and other contortions to squeeze the program into the do-while mold.

Compare the DO block with exit version with the do-while pseudocode version. The only drawback of the Fortran 77 DO block with exit version is the labels, which may become unnecessary in some future revision of the Fortran standard. The drawback of the do-while version is the duplication of code, which is inherent in the do-while structure.

Vocabulary

DO block
DO loop
DO variable
do-while block
echo of input data
exit
function definition, one-line
hand simulation
label
loop body
nested DO blocks
statement function
step size

Chapter Outline

Examination Questions

Part One: True or False

Indicate which of the sentences below are true, and which are false. If a sentence is false, explain what is wrong

1. In Fortran 77, a DO variable may be type real.

2. A DO block begins with a DO statement and ends with an END statement.

3. The label in the DO statement heading a DO block must agree with the label on the CONTINUE statement ending the DO block.

4. A DO block can be executed no times if the expressions in the DO statement so specify.

5. The step size in a DO block may be negative.

Part Two: Multiple Choice

Choose the one best answer.

1. The normal number of iterations of a DO block

   a. is fixed when the program is written.
   b. cannot change after execution of the program begins.
   c. is determined by the values of variables when the block is entered.
   d. can be changed within the loop by calculating a new stopping value.
   e. must be specified by constants or parameters.

2. Numeric statement labels are used in Fortran

   a. because Fortran evolved from BASIC.
   b. because alphabetic statement labels weren't invented until much later.
   c. because early computer could not read alphabetic information.
   d. because they must be in increasing numerical order.
   e. none of the above.

3. A DO block with exit is

   a. always executed the full number of times specified in the DO statement.
   b. always exited before the full number of iterations specified in the DO statement.
   c. cheating because the DO statement has no real effect.
   d. usually exited by a GO TO statement when a test condition is met.
   e. none of the above.

4. Loops are important in computer programming because

   a. they create many bugs.
   b. they allow the computer to choose between alternative computational steps.
   c. they allow some statements in a program to be executed more than once.
   d. they show how computers can solve many problems in the real world.
   e. none of the above.

5. The Fortran statement: SUM = SUM + SCORE

   a. reads a new value for the variable SCORE.
   b. reads a new value for the variable SUM.
   c. expresses the mathematical identity that SCORE = 0.
   d. increases the value of SUM by the current value of SCORE.
   e. changes the values of both SUM and SCORE.

Part Three: Syntax

Indicate which of the following Fortran programs or sequences of statements are syntactically correct, and which are not. If a program or statement is not correct, rewrite it to make it correct, or indicate why this is not possible. Be sure not to change the "intent" of the statement in the process of correcting the syntax. Assume all variables are correctly declared.

1.
```
      DO 18 I = 1, 10
         COUNT = COUNT + 1
      CONTINUE
```

2.
```
      DO 18 I = 1, 10, J
         COUNT = COUNT + J
   18 CONTINUE
```

3.
```
      DO 28 J = 100, 1
         PRINT *, J
   28 CONTINUE
```

4.
```
      SUM = 0
      DO 18 ROW = 1, 10
         DO 28 COL = 1, 50
            PROD = ROW * COL
            PRINT *, PROD
            SUM = SUM + PROD
   18    CONTINUE
   28 CONTINUE
```

5.
```
      FNF (X) =  X * X
      FOR X = 2, 10, 2
         PRINT *, X, FNF (X)
   10 CONTINUE
```

Part Four: Output

What output will be printed when the following programs are run? If the output is formatted, use *b*'s to clearly indicate the blank columns in the output.

1.
```
      PROGRAM ONE
      INTEGER M, N
      DO 18 M = 1, 10
         DO 28 N = 1, 10
            IF (N .EQ. M ** 2) THEN
               PRINT *, M, N
            END IF
   28    CONTINUE
   18 CONTINUE
      END
```

2.
```
      PROGRAM TWO
      INTEGER P, Q, R
```

```
      READ *, Q
      READ *, P
      DO 18 N = 1, 100
         R = Q
         Q = P
         READ *, P
         PRINT *, 'INPUT DATA  P: ', P
         IF (P .EQ. Q) THEN
            PRINT *, R
            GO TO 19
         END IF
   18 CONTINUE
   19 END
```

3.

```
      PROGRAM THREE
      INTEGER SUM, NUM
      SUM = 0
      DO 18 NUM = 10, 100, 10
         SUM = SUM + NUM
         PRINT *, 'NUM = ', NUM, '      SUM = ', SUM
   18 CONTINUE
      PRINT *, 'FINAL SUM IS ', SUM
      END
```

4.

```
      PROGRAM FOUR
      INTEGER COUNT
      REAL A, B, C, D, SUM, TOT1, TOT3, TOT5
      TOT1 = 0
      TOT3 = 0
      TOT5 = 0
      DO 18 COUNT = 1, 4
         READ *, A, B, C, D
         SUM = A + B + C + D
         PRINT '(5F10.5)', A, B, C, D, SUM
         TOT1 = TOT1 + A
         TOT3 = TOT3 + C
         TOT5 = TOT5 + SUM
   18 CONTINUE
      PRINT '(3F10.5)', TOT1, TOT3, TOT5
      END
```

Part Five: Programming

1. The Problem: An integer greater than 1 is considered a prime number if it has no factors except 1 and itself. Thus 2, 3, 5, 7, and 11 are prime numbers, but $6 = 2 \times 3$ and $15 = 3 \times 5$ are not prime numbers. A number which has factors other than 1 and itself is a composite numbers. Write a computer program that reads a number as input and decides whether it is prime or composite by testing all possible candidates for factors. The Output: If a number is prime, print a message saying so; if a number is composite, print one set of factors.

2. The Problem: Write a program to calculate the cubes of successive integers: 1, 8, 27, 64, 125, ... Your program should print only the first number whose cube is greater than 10000, and it should also print what the cube is. For extra credit, also print the largest number whose cube is less than 10000.

Answer Key

Part One: True or False

1. True.

2. False, it usually ends with a CONTINUE statement

3. True.

4. True.

5. True.

Part Two: Multiple Choice

1. c.

2. e, assembler languages used alphabetic labels before Fortran was invented.

3. d.

4. c.

5. d.

Part Three: Syntax

1.
```
      DO 18 I = 1, 10
         COUNT = COUNT + 1
   18 CONTINUE                        <--missing label
```
2.
```
      DO 18 I = 1, 10, J              <--correct DO block
         COUNT = COUNT + J
   18 CONTINUE
```
3.
```
      DO 28 J = 100, 1               <--syntax if OK, but executes 0 times
         PRINT *, J
   28 CONTINUE
```
4.
```
      SUM = 0
      DO 18 ROW = 1, 10
         DO 28 COL = 1, 50
            PROD = ROW * COL
            PRINT *, PROD
            SUM = SUM + PROD
   28      CONTINUE                   <--improper nesting of
   18 CONTINUE                        <--DO blocks (labels 18 and 28)
```
5.
```
      FNF (X) = X * X                 <--correct function definition stmt
      DO 10 X = 2, 10, 2              <--keyword DO; this isn't BASIC
         PRINT *, X, FNF (X)
   10 CONTINUE
```

Part Four: Output

1.
```
      1      1
      2      4
      3      9
```

2.

```
RUN TWO
INPUT DATA  P:        3
INPUT DATA  P:        4
INPUT DATA  P:        5
INPUT DATA  P:        5
         4
```

3.

```
RUN THREE
NUM =       10    SUM =        10
NUM =       20    SUM =        30
NUM =       30    SUM =        60
NUM =       40    SUM =       100
NUM =       50    SUM =       150
NUM =       60    SUM =       210
NUM =       70    SUM =       280
NUM =       80    SUM =       360
NUM =       90    SUM =       450
NUM =      100    SUM =       550
FINAL SUM IS      550
```

4.

```
RUN FOUR
    1.20000    2.30000    3.40000    4.50000   11.40000
    1.20000   -2.30000    3.40000   -4.50000   -2.20000
   -1.20000    2.30000   -3.40000    4.50000    2.20000
   10.20000   10.30000   10.40000   10.50000   41.40000
   11.40000   13.80000   52.80000
```

Part Five: Programming:

1.

```
      PROGRAM PRIME
C     TESTS WHETHER A NUMBER IS PRIME OR COMPOSITE
      INTEGER N, TEST, INTQUO, FACT1, FACT2
      READ *, N
      PRINT *, 'INPUT DATA  N: ', N
      FACT1 = 1
      DO 18 TEST = 2, N-1
         INTQUO = N / TEST
         IF (N .EQ. INTQUO * TEST) THEN
            FACT1 = TEST
            FACT2 = INTQUO
            GOTO 19
         END IF
   18 CONTINUE
   19 IF (FACT1 .EQ. 1) THEN
         PRINT *, 'THE NUMBER ', N, ' IS PRIME'
      ELSE
         PRINT *, 'THE NUMBER ', N, ' IS COMPOSITE'
         PRINT *, 'TWO FACTORS ARE ', FACT1, ' AND ', FACT2
      END IF
      END
```

```
RUN PRIME
INPUT DATA  N:       107
THE NUMBER     107 IS PRIME

RUN PRIME
INPUT DATA  N:     1111
THE NUMBER    1111 IS COMPOSITE
TWO FACTORS ARE       11 AND      101
```

2.

```
      PROGRAM CUBE
C     FINDS THE FIRST NUMBER WHOSE CUBE EXCEEDS 10000
      INTEGER NUM
      DO 18 NUM = 1, 10000
         IF (NUM ** 3 .GT. 10000) THEN
            GOTO 19
         END IF
   18 CONTINUE
   19 PRINT *, NUM, ' CUBED EXCEEDS 10000'
      PRINT *, NUM, ' ** 3 = ', NUM ** 3
      PRINT *
      PRINT *, NUM - 1, ' IS THE LAST NUMBER WHOSE CUBE < 10000'
      PRINT *, NUM - 1, ' ** 3 = ', (NUM - 1) ** 3
      END
```

```
RUN CUBE
    22 CUBED EXCEEDS 10000
    22 ** 3 =    10648

    21 IS THE LAST NUMBER WHOSE CUBE < 10000
    21 ** 3 =     9261
```

SUBPROGRAMS, MODULARITY, AND STEPWISE REFINEMENT 5

Argument Passing

Argument passing is probably the hardest topic in the entire course, judging from the relative difficulty our students have with it. The approach we favor is a two-step introduction to subroutines (and function subprograms). For the first go-round, we adopt the simplified convention that the argument lists in the CALL statement and in the SUBROUTINE statement should be identical in every respect. This means that exactly the same variable names are used in the calling programs as in the subroutine and that they are listed in the same order. It also means that the declarations for these variables must be identical in both places.

Independence of Subprograms

The second fact a student needs to know about subprograms is that each subroutine is independent of each other subroutine and of the main program. This means that all variables must be redeclared in a subprogram. (The default type conventions sometimes avert catastrophes caused by omitted declarations, and sometimes cause the catastrophes.)

In addition, the independence of subprograms means that values that are to be shared between calling program and subprogram must be listed in the argument lists of the subprogram call. It is common for beginners to omit a variable and wonder why the answers do not make their way back.

Special Debugging Techniques for Subprogram Calls

Subprograms call for a new debugging technique to test the passing of arguments. If there is doubt that the relevant input values to a subprogram are being made available to the subprogram or that the answers are being passed back to the calling program, well placed PRINT statements can show what is happening.

It is not sufficient to print the values of the supplied arguments before the subprogram call; the values of the dummy arguments (actual arguments) should also be printed immediately upon entering the subprogram. Any mistake in argument passing to the subprogram will be revealed by this technique. Similarly, not only should the values of the answers be printed when they are calculated in the subprogram, they should also be printed right after the CALL statement in the calling program to see if they made it back to the calling program.

Why Use Subroutines?

The old answer used to be to save lines of code. If the same sequence of Fortran statements is used in several different places in a program, then the program can be shortened by making the common statements a subroutine and replacing each instance of these statements with a subroutine call.

The better answer is that a properly modularized program is easier to read, easier to debug, easier to modify, and more likely to be correct. Using subroutines is a natural consequence of the top-down program planning philosophy. Pseudocode statements at one level of refinement become subroutines at the next level of refinement.

The Gradepoint Case Study

With this case study, we graduate from "toy" programs to "real" programs. Not that the quadratic formula or the escape velocity of a rocket or income tax or the trapezoidal approximation to an integral are not real problems, only that the programs to solve them are short. When the size of a program increases by an order of magnitude, writing the program requires not just more of the same kinds of techniques, it requires new techniques to cope with the sheer size of the task.

That new technique is top-down program design, which gets its first full scale test in this chapter. In the gradepoint case study, none of the individual pieces is as important as the organization of the task into pieces.

Arrays

It is really hard to program a meaningful problem without arrays, so we "cheat" a little and introduce them a chapter early. A student takes more than one course, gets more than one grade, etc. Each of these calls for a list or array: a list of courses, a list of grades, etc. We find very little difficulty getting across the idea that TITLE stands for the full list of course titles and that TITLE (3) stands for the title of the 3rd course.

Documentation

A certain way to get everyone mad at you is to start preaching about the "right" amount of documentation. Industry standards and individual taste vary, and everyone is certain he or she is right.

The level of documentation acceptable in a student program, one of 5 or 10 submitted in a semester or quarter, should not be the same as the level of documentation expected in a production program that will be in service for several years. There simply isn't enough time for it.

Since most students tend to underdocument, we first talk about abuses in that direction. Cryptic variable names are fundamentally unacceptable. Make your students use self-explanatory names. If a suitable variable name cannot be found using only 6 characters, document what the name means in a comment statement.

Pseudocode statements which have been refined to several Fortran statements make excellent headings to document the purpose of the group of Fortran statements.

Occasionally a student gets the idea that the instructor likes documentation, the more the better, and that student proceeds to document every line of code. To such a student we point out the sin of overdocumentation. Never put a comment that says exactly the same thing as the line of code it documents. Never explain that the variable SUM is the sum and COST is the cost. Self-explanatory variable names do not need explaining.

Cryptic steps do need explaining in the program listing, but it is better yet to use a cleaner algorithm that does not have the cryptic steps.

When To Document

All too often, a student comes for help with a program, and you notice that there are no comments in it at all. "Oh, I was going to put in lots of comments before I submit the program," the student says. The reason for putting comments in a program is not to impress the instructor and improve the grade (although this reason is a strong motivating force that can be put to the instructor's advantage), it is to help write and debug the program. For most programs, the time it takes to insert helpful comments will be more than repaid before the debugging is finished. Good documentation pays off in the short run as well as the long run.

Subroutines vs. Functions

The basic syntactic difference between a subroutine and a function subprogram is that a subroutine is called explicitly in a separate statement, a CALL statement, whereas a function subprogram is called implicitly by using the function in an expression.

In the mathematical tradition from which Fortran derives, a function computes a single value, the function value. Thus, in the mathematical tradition, a Fortran function subprogram should return one value (through the function name) and should not change the values of its arguments.

Certain other programming languages, such as C, do not make a distinction between functions and subroutines. In C, everything is a function. Thus, C programmers are in the habit of seeing functions whose purpose is to pass back values through the argument list. As long time Fortran programmers, we have never quite gotten used to having the statement

```
Y = F (X)
```

walk the dog, take in the laundry, and milk the cow, as well as calculate the function value, F (X). We find it confusing.

Array Declarations in a Subprogram

In a main program, an array must be declared with constant subscript bounds. If the data for the array are really variable length, the maximum expected subscript is used in the main program declaration.

Subprogram array declarations, on the other hand, can be written in a way that allows them to be used with any main program declarations for the corresponding arrays. Dummy variables and integer valued expressions in the dummy variables, can be used in the declaration of subscript bounds. Thus, if the calling program is asked to pass the declared subscript bounds as well as the name of an array, the subprogram does not have to declare a fixed length for the array.

For a singly subscripted array, there is no harm in a subprogram declaring a smaller number of elements that its calling program. Thus, for variable length data, if the subprogram does not increase the number of array elements with actual data in them, the subprogram can declare the actual length of the array data rather than the maximum length.

Reinventing the Wheel

The subroutines READLI (read a list of integers), PRNTLI (print a list of integers), and SWAPI (swap integers) are the start of a collection of generally useful subroutines that, written in sufficient generality, will serve the programmer in good stead in future programs. In one sense, programmer-defined subroutines and procedures, like built-in functions, form extensions of the Fortran language. Once written and debugged, they can form part of the programmer's vocabulary. They represent pseudocode statements whose refinement is already written.

A library of useful subroutines is one way to keep from reinventing the wheel in every program. To get the idea across, we sometimes tell a joke about some experiments to distinguish between an engineer and a mathematician.

The Difference Between an Engineer and a Mathematician

The supplies for these experiments are some kindling, some matches, a bucket, and a supply of water. You will also need two adjoining rooms.

Experiment 1, part 1. You are in one room, and the engineer is in the other. You set a fire in your room, you place a full bucket of water at the right of the fire, and you shout, "Fire!". The engineer will rush into your room, diagnose the problem, grab the bucket of water from the right of the fire, extinguish the fire, and then return to the other room to go back to work.

Experiment 1, part 2. You are in one room, and the mathematician is in the other. You set a fire in your room, you place a full bucket of water at the right of the fire, and you shout "Fire!". The mathematician will rush into your room, diagnose the problem, grab the bucket of water from the right of the fire, extinguish the fire, and then return to the other room to go back to work.

Experiment 2, part 1. Once again, you are in one room, and the engineer is in the other. Once again you set a fire in your room, but this time you place a full bucket of water at the *left* of the fire, and you then shout "Fire!". The engineer will rush into your room, diagnose the problem, grab the bucket of water from the left of the fire, extinguish the fire, and then leave to go back to work.

Experiment 2, part 2. Once again, you are in one room, and the mathematician is in the other. You set a fire in your room, and as in the second stage for the engineer, this time you place a bucket of water at the *left* of the fire, and you shout, "Fire!". The mathematician will rush into your room, diagnose the problem, grab the bucket of water from the left of the fire, and move the bucket to the *right* of the fire. Having reduced the new problem to one that has already been solved, the mathematician will leave the room and go back to work.

In writing programs, unlike stopping fires, it is nearly always desirable to solve a new problem by calling a previously written subroutine. Don't reinvent the wheel every time. Helping your students to remember the principle of reusing old subroutines to solve new problems is a good reason to tell the joke.

Vocabulary

actual argument
argument
argument passing
array
array declaration
CALL statement
documentation
dummy argument
external documentation
function
function subprogram
function value assignment
internal documentation
local variable
manual for use of a program
modularity
module
nested subprogram calls
reference argument
self-documenting
side effect
subprogram
subprogram call
subroutine
subscript
successive refinement
supplied argument
target language
termination signal
top-down analysis
value argument

Chapter Outline

Examination Questions

Part One: True or False

Indicate which of the sentences below are true and which are false. If a sentence is false, explain what is wrong.

1. A subroutine is called in the same way as a function subprogram.

2. A dummy argument must have the same type as the corresponding supplied or actual argument.

3. Arrays are permitted as dummy arguments.

4. Constants and parameters are permitted as dummy arguments.

5. In top-down program design, the first subroutine executed is the first subroutine written.

Part Two: Multiple Choice

Choose one best answer.

1. A dummy argument is

    a. a variable in a program.
    b. an argument between two stupid people.
    c. a parameter.
    d. written in parentheses in a CALL statement.
    e. written in parentheses in a SUBROUTINE statement.

2. If a variable in a subroutine has the same name as a variable in the main program,

    a. the variable must appear in the argument list of the subroutine call.
    b. The variable need not be declared in the subroutine.
    c. the variable must be declared in the subroutine but not the main program.
    d. the variables need not represent the same value in both places.
    e. any change of the value of the variable in the subroutine will change the value of the variable in the main program.

3. If an actual argument is a variable name

    a. the corresponding dummy argument may be a constant or expression.
    b. the argument is passed by value.
    c. the argument is passed by reference.
    d. no information may be returned through this argument.
    e. a and d above.

4. If an array is compared to a street, in the same analogy a subscript corresponds to

    a. an avenue.
    b. a city.
    c. a house number on the street.
    d. the electric, gas, and water utilities that service the street.
    e. a person who lives on the street.

5. A function subprogram

    a. is limited to a single statement defining the function value.
    b. is called with a CALL statement.
    c. cannot use the same variable names as the main program.
    d. contains all the declarations necessary to compile it separately from the main program.

e.   must use the same variable names as the main program.

Part Three: Syntax

Indicate which of the following Fortran programs or sequence of statements are syntactically correct, and which are not. If a program or statement is not correct, rewrite it to make it correct, or indicate why this is not possible. Be sure not to change the "intent" of the statement in the process of correcting the syntax. Assume all variables are correctly declared.

1.

```
SUBROUTINE F (A, B, C)
REAL A, B, C
A = B + C
RETURN
```

2.

```
FUNCTION MEAN (X, Y, Z)
REAL X, Y, Z
MEAN = (X + Y + Z) / 3
F (X) = MEAN
END
```

3.

```
PROGRAM AVG (A, ANS)
REAL A (1:100) ANS
CALL READ (A)
CALL PRINT (A)
CALL AVG (A, ANS)
PRINT *, 'THE AVERAGE IS ', AVG
CALL END
```

4.

```
PROGRAM SUM
REAL SUM, A (1:100)
CALL READLR (A)
CALL READLR (B)
SUM = F (A) + F (B)
PRINT *, SUM
END
```

5.

```
PROGRAM CUBE
READ *, N
ANS = CUBE (N) / CUBE (2.0)
PRINT 'THE ANSWER IS ', ANS

FUNCTION CUBE (N, 2)
REAL *, N, CUBE
CUBE = (ABS (N)) ** 3
IF (N < 0) THEN
   CUBE = - CUBE
END IF
END
```

Part Four: Output

What output will be printed when the following programs are run? If the output is formatted, use *b*'s to clearly indicate the blank columns in the output.

1.

```
     PROGRAM ONE
     INTEGER N
     DO 18 N = 5, 1, -1
        CALL UPTO (N)
  18 CONTINUE
     END

     SUBROUTINE UPTO (P)
     INTEGER N, P
     DO 18 N = 1, P
        PRINT '(I5)', N
  18 CONTINUE
     END
```

2.

```
     PROGRAM TWO
     REAL F
     PRINT '(F15.5)', F (8, 3)
     END

     FUNCTION F (X, Y)
     INTEGER X, Y
     REAL F
     F = G (X) / (G (Y) * G (X - Y))
     END

     FUNCTION G (X)
     INTEGER G, X, N, PROD
     PROD = 1
     DO 18 N = 1, X
        PROD = PROD * N
  18 CONTINUE
     END
```

Part Five: Programming

1. The Problem: A popular microcomputer has a peculiar memory map for locations on its display screen. The display screen has 24 lines numbered from 0 to 23 and 40 characters on each line. The column numbers run from 0 to 39. The memory address of the character in line LINE and column COL is found by adding the column number COL to the address of the first character on the line. For lines 0 to 7, the address of the first character on the line is given by the formula

```
     1024 + 128 * LINE
```

For lines 8 to 15, the address is given by the formula

```
     1024 + 128 * (LINE - 8) + 40
```

For lines 16 to 23, the address of the first character is given by the formula

```
     1024 + 128 * (LINE - 16) + 80
```

Write a program that reads as input a line number from 0 to 23 and a column number from 0 to 39, and which prints the memory address of that position on the display screen. You must use a function subprogram to calculate the address and another function subprogram to calculate the address of the beginning of a line on the display screen. Sample Execution:

```
RUN ADDRES
INPUT DATA  LINE: 12
            COL:  15
MEMORY ADDRESS = 1591
```

Answer Key

Part One: True or False

1. False, a subroutine call uses a CALL statement and a function call just uses the function in an (arithmetic) expression.

2. True.

3. True.

4. False, dummy arguments must be variables. Constants and parameters are permitted as actual arguments.

5. False.

Part Two: Multiple Choice

1. e.

2. d. Answer e is true only if the variable appears both as dummy argument and as corresponding actual argument in the subroutine call.

3. c.

4. c. Answer e is the common mistake of confusing an address (subscript) with the contents of that address.

5. d. Answer a is a better description of the statement function, the one-line definition of a function in the main program than it is of a function subprogram.

Part Three: Syntax

1.
```
      SUBROUTINE F (A, B, C)
      REAL A, B, C
      A = B + C
      RETURN              <--RETURN is optional; we would omit it
      END                 <--missing END statement
```

2.
```
      FUNCTION MEAN (X, Y, Z)
      REAL X, Y, Z, MEAN     <--function name should be declared
      MEAN = (X + Y + Z) / 3

                             <--deleted nonsense statement

      END
```

3.
```
      PROGRAM AVG                <--no argument list for a main program
      REAL A (1:100), ANS        <--missing comma
      CALL READ (A)              <--correct statements; keywords are not
      CALL PRINT (A)                 not reserved in Fortran
      CALL FNDAVG (A, ANS)       <--duplicate name changed
      PRINT *, 'THE AVERAGE IS ', ANS   <--a subroutine name has no value
      END                        <--deleted keyword CALL
```

4.
```
      PROGRAM SUM                <--correct program, assuming subroutines
      REAL SUM, A (1:100)            and function will be supplied.
      CALL READLR (A)
      CALL READLR (B)
      SUM = F (A) + F (B)
```

```
      PRINT *, SUM
      END
```

5.

```
      PROGRAM CUBE
      REAL N, CUBE, ANS                <--missing declarations; defaults are
      READ *, N                                 not sufficiently consistent
      ANS = CUBE (N) / CUBE (2.0)
      PRINT *, 'THE ANSWER IS ', ANS   <--missing * format
      END                              <--missing END statement

      FUNCTION CUBE (N)                <--wrong number of arguments
      REAL N, CUBE                     <--careless slip of the mind
      CUBE = (ABS (N)) ** 3
      IF ( N .LT. 0) THEN              <--wrong symbol for comparison
         CUBE = - CUBE
      END IF
      END
```

Part Four: Output

1.

```
      1
      2
      3
      4
      5
      1
      2
      3
      4
      1
      2
      3
      1
      2
      1
```

The duplicated labels and variable name in subroutine and main program
are intended to confuse the insecure student.

2.

```
      56.00000
```

G (X) is the factorial function and F(X, Y) is the number of ways of
choosing Y members from a set of X objects.

Part Five: Programming

1.

```
      PROGRAM ADDRES
C     FINDS THE ADDRESS OF A PARTICULAR LINE AND COLUMN ON THE DISPLAY SCREEN
C     OF A POPULAR MICROCOMPUTER
      INTEGER LINE, COL, ADDR

      READ *, LINE, COL
      PRINT *, 'INPUT DATA  LINE: ', LINE
      PRINT *, '            COL: ', COL
```

```
      PRINT *, 'MEMORY ADDRESS = ', ADDR (LINE, COL)
      END

      FUNCTION ADDR (LINE, COL)
      INTEGER ADDR, LINE, COL, LINBEG
      ADDR = LINBEG (LINE) + COL
      END

      FUNCTION LINBEG (LINE)
      INTEGER LINBEG, LINE, BASE
      PARAMETER (BASE = 1024)
      IF (LINE .LE. 7) THEN
         LINBEG = BASE + 128 * LINE
      ELSE IF (8 .LE. LINE  .AND.  LINE .LE. 15) THEN
         LINBEG = BASE + 128 * (LINE - 8) + 40
      ELSE
         LINBEG = BASE + 128 * (LINE - 16) + 80
      END IF
      END
```

```
RUN ADDRES
INPUT DATA  LINE:  12
            COL:   15
MEMORY ADDRESS =   1591
```

ARRAYS 6

Students in the humanities and social sciences sometimes find arrays difficult. The conceptual difficulty seems to be the problem of distinguishing the value of the subscript I from the value of the array element A(I). By way of contrast, arrays are easy for mathematics, science, and engineering majors, because they are already familiar with subscripted variable notations.

Describing How Arrays Are Implemented

Once students learn how arrays are implemented in a computer, they usually understand the underlying concept of subscripted variables as well. A list is implemented, most of the time, as a sequence of adjacent memory locations. The array name A is regarded as a "base address", and the subscript I gives the offset, or relative address. Figure 6.1 in the text illustrates a 1-dimensional array in computer memory.

If you want to start with something simpler, you might mention the mundane analogy that an array name A is like a street, and the subscript I is like a house number on the street.

Advantages of Arrays in List Processing

Once students see how arrays can enable them to do things they couldn't do before, they will understand the concept. In particular, arrays will make it possible for your students to read in a list as input and then print it out in reverse order. Without arrays, what a pain it would be to do this with a list of variable length up to, say, 100 items.

Another good exercise for students is to write a program that reads an arbitrarily long list, waits for a termination signal, and then prints the last ten items in the list. Without arrays, this could be like giving the directions, "Watch where I get off the bus, and you get off ten stops sooner."

It helps to point out that applications like searching and sorting would be dreadful to program if it were not for arrays. You might also mention that within a few months on their first job, most college graduates are saying, "We want arrays!" (If you have any doubt about this assertion, just read it aloud— if you got it immediately, pardon us for explaining.)

Algorithms for Searching

Careful discussion and comparison of the various algorithms for searching can be the high point of the entire course for the students who are going to take courses beyond introductions to languages. For substantial applications like searching, the design or choice of an algorithm is far more important to the overall cost effectiveness than anything else.

In particular, the algorithm itself is more important to cost savings than whether the programmer knows and uses every last special detail of a programming language. Beginning students often need to be told that explicitly.

Doing a two-level search is like using "fast forward" on an audio tape to locate the approximate beginning of a selection. Viewed another way, why look ahead one item at a time when you can look ahead 100 items at a time. Of course, if you skip too far ahead at each step, it may be time-consuming to complete the search in the gaps.

The optimal two-level search of a list of length n is based on approximately $\sqrt{n}$ pages of $\sqrt{n}$ items each. It is a good exercise for students who have had calculus to prove the optimality of $\sqrt{n} \times \sqrt{n}$ partitioning.

Why Should Computer Programmers Understand Some Mathematics?

It is easy to demonstrate that when you sequentially search an ordered list of 1,000,000 items, a two-level search is more efficient than a one-level search, that three levels are more efficient than two, four levels are more efficient than three, and so on. Well, not quite. A million levels is not as efficient as two levels.

This is an opportunity to demonstrate a simple relationship between mathematics and computer science. There is no efficiency to be gained from increasing the number of levels of search beyond the logarithm base 2 of the list length. (Calculus gives a similar result using logarithms base e, but the number of items in each level is so small that the continuity assumptions on which calculus is based are not quite satisfied.)

About Sorting

If you have an above average class, you can extend Section 6.4 by telling your students about merge sorting. If you are preparing them for a data structures and algorithms course, you might at some point also discuss quicksort. It is never too early to learn of the power of divide and conquer methods.

Testing and Debugging

Arrays provide not only new computing power, but also new opportunities to make mistakes. Depending on the size of your class, you can assign the testing and debugging section as required reading, or present it as an unfolding mystery using an overhead projector to flash the sample output on the screen in each stage of the debugging process.

If you are really sure of yourself, and the equipment is available, there are large screen projectors that can be driven off a computer. Then, you can actually do the debugging examples "live", complete with unintended errors that inevitably get introduced when you type in real time in front of the class. Careful planning and thorough familiarity with most of the things that can go wrong are a must for anyone attempting this kind of demonstration, but the results are worth it.

Vocabulary

array
array declaration
binary search
DATA statement
default file
divide and conquer
efficiency
EQUIVALENCE statement
file
implied DO loop
index variable
interchange sort
list
list of character strings
multi-level search
one-dimensional array
OPEN statement
ordered list
page
READ statement
search
sequential search
simple variable
sort
subscript out of bounds
subscript
two-level search
unit number
vector
variable length list
WRITE statement

Chapter Outline

Examination Questions

Part One: True or False

Indicate which of the sentences below are true and which are false. If a sentence is false, explain what is wrong.

1. Arrays are declared of fixed length in Fortran.

2. Sequential search is the best possible search method because no items are skipped.

3. It takes about the same amount of time to sort a list as to search it.

4. A binary search scans a list two elements at a time.

5. A list of character strings has two subscripts.

Part Two: Multiple Choice

Choose one best answer.

1. For calculating an average of a list of integers, an advantage of using an array instead of reusing the same integer variable is that

    a. the array uses less memory than an integer variable.
    b. there is a built-in function AVG that works on arrays only.
    c. only with an array can the input data be echoed.
    d. all the data are accessible for later use in the program.
    e. none of the above.

2. The subscript of an array must be

    a. an integer variable.
    b. an integer variable, constant, or parameter.
    c. an integer valued expression
    d. greater than zero.
    e. c and d above.

3. One _____ declare an array REAL A (1.0 : 10.0) _____.

    a. cannot; because the "." would cause a syntax error.
    b. cannot; because there are an infinite number of reals between 1.0 and 10.0.
    c. can; as long as 1.0 and 10.0 are declared as parameters.
    d. can; since the bounds are both positive integers.
    e. cannot; because the step size was omitted in the subscript range.

4. Before you use a binary search you

    a. must make sure the length of the list is an even number.
    b. must make sure the list is sorted.
    c. should use a sequential search first, and then use the binary search only if the sequential search proves inefficient.
    d. must make sure that no value appears twice in the list, as that will create ambiguity that the binary search cannot handle.
    e. must extend the list until its length is a power of two because the binary search works for no other list sizes.

5. A list may be sorted by

    a. successively finding the smallest remaining element.
    b. placing the first smallest element first, the second smallest second, ..., and the nth smallest nth.

    c. randomly scrambling the list, and then testing to see if it is in sorted order.

    d. separating it into a low half and a high half, and then sorting each half.

    e. all of the above.

6. Sorting _____ than searching.

    a. is, on the average, faster
    b. is, on the average, slower
    c. may be faster
    d. is more efficient
    e. produces fewer errors

7. Using the most efficient algorithm, the maximum number of tries it takes to guess a number in the range 1 to 64, with certainty of getting it right—you are told with each try whether you are too high, too low, or exactly right—is

    a. 64
    b. 32, which is the average of the numbers 1, 2, 3, ..., 64
    c. 7
    d. 6
    e. 1

8. Negative subscripts are

    a. useful because there aren't enough positive integers.
    b. useful because they avoid the problems of subscript zero.
    c. are forbidden in Fortran.
    d. should never be used if there are positive subscripts available.
    e. none of the above.

9. Multi-level searches achieve their efficiency by

    a. examining more than one element at a time.
    b. looking at only one letter or digit of an entry on each pass.
    c. splitting a list in two or more parts with each comparison.
    d. skipping rapidly through the list without examining each element until the very last level.
    e. working only on sorted lists.

10. The implied DO loop is needed because

    a. the applied DO loop has too many restrictions.
    b. the DO block cannot be used in a subroutine.
    c. the DO block cannot be used in a DATA statement.
    d. each PRINT statement starts a new line of output.
    e. c and d above.

Part Three: Syntax

Which of the following array declarations are correct? Correct the ones that are not correct. Do not change the "intent" of the declarations in the process of correcting them. If a declaration cannot be corrected, tell why.

1.

```
REAL A (1:100), B(1:100), C(1:10)
```

2.

```
INTEGER PRIME (1:10), NUMBER (20), FACTOR (0:5)
```

3.

```
CHARACTER NAME (1:10) *25
```

4.
```
      LIST (-20 : 20), RESULT (-20 : 20)
```
5.
```
      INTEGER SKIP2 (2:10:2)
```

Part Four: Output

What output will be printed when the following programs are run? If the output is formatted, use b's to clearly indicate the blank columns in the output.

1.
```
      PROGRAM ONE
      INTEGER A (1:10), I
      DO 18 I = 1, 10
         A (I) = I ** 2
   18 CONTINUE
      DO 28 I = 10, 1, -2
         PRINT *, A (I)
   28 CONTINUE
      END
```

2.
```
      PROGRAM TWO
      INTEGER A (1:10), I
      DATA (A (I), I = 1, 10) / 2, 3, 5, 7, 11, 13, 17, 19 23, 29 /
      DO 18 I = 2, 10, 2
         PRINT *, A (I)
   18 CONTINUE
      END
```

3.
```
      PROGRAM THREE
      INTEGER A (-5 : 5), I, LOOK
      DATA (A (I), I = -5, 5) / 1, 3, 5, 7, 9, 11, 13, 14, 15, 17, 19 /
      READ *, LOOK
      PRINT *, 'INPUT DATA  LOOK: ', LOOK
      DO 18 I = 1, 5
         IF (A (I) .EQ. LOOK) THEN
            PRINT *, 'FOUND: ', I
         END IF
   18 CONTINUE
```
   a. For the first run use the input value 5 for LOOK.
   b. For the second run use the input value 15 for LOOK.

4.
```
      PROGRAM FOUR
      INTEGER A (1 : 5), I, J, B
      DO 18 I = 1, 5
         READ *, A(I)
   18 CONTINUE
      DO 28 I = 1, 4
         DO 38 J = I+1, 5
            IF (A (I) .LT. A(J)) THEN
               B = A (I)
               A (I) = A (J)
               A (J) = B
```

```
         END IF
38   CONTINUE
28 CONTINUE
   PRINT '(5I3)', (A (I), I = 1, 5)
   END
```

The input file consists of the following numbers.

```
44
33
17
85
12
```

5.

```
   PROGRAM FIVE
   INTEGER A (1 : 8), B (1 : 4), I, SUM1, SUM2
   READ *, (A (I), I = 1, 8)
   SUM1 = 0
   DO 18 I = 1, 4
      SUM1 = SUM1 + A (I)
18 CONTINUE
   SUM2 = 0
   DO 28 I = 5, 8
      SUM2 = SUM2 + A (I)
28 CONTINUE
   IF (SUM1 .GT. SUM2) THEN
      DO 38 I = 1, 4
         B (I) = A (I)
38    CONTINUE
   ELSE
      DO 48 I = 1, 4
         B (I) = A (4 + I)
48    CONTINUE
   END IF
   PRINT '(2(/, 2I3))', (B (I), I = 1, 4)
   END
```

The input file consists of the following line:

```
1, 9, 2, 8, 3, 7, 4, 6
```

Part Five: Programming

1. The Problem: Any positive integer of up to 101 decimal digits can be represented as the values of an integer array DIGIT (0 : 100) in which DIGIT (N) is the decimal digit of the number whose place value is 10 to the power N. Thus the number 123 is represented by DIGIT (0) = 3, DIGIT (1) = 2, DIGIT (2) = 1, and all other values in the array DIGIT are zero. Using this kind of representation, very large integers can be represented. Write a program to read the values of two such numbers and to print each number and their sum in ordinary decimal notation. Addition should be done the way you learned in grade school. Add the digits starting at the units place and working toward higher place values. If the sum in any place exceeds 9, then subtract 10 from the sum in that place and carry it to the next higher place. Input Data: Because of the variable length of the input numbers, they will be present least significant digit first, followed by increasingly more significant digits until finally a signal of -1 follows the

highest order nonzero digit. For example, the number 32,768 is given in the input data by the six numbers

8, 6, 7, 2, 3, −1

Sample Output:

RUN SUM

```
        12345678901234566789
         2626262626262613
        --------------------
        1237194152749719402
```

Leading blanks in the smaller numbers may be printed as leading zeros, but don't print all 101 digits.

2. The Problem: Using the same representations as in problem 1, write a program to multiply two large integers. Only the two integers and the product need be shown, not the intermediate sums used in the hand method. Sample Output:

RUN PROD

```
        00000000000000001234567891234567890
        00000000000000000002626262626262613
        -----------------------------------
        3242299509415122668205659271729657
```

Answer Key

Part One: True or False

1. True

2. False, it may even be the worst search method because not items are skipped.

3. False, using efficient algorithms for each, sorting takes longer than searching.

4. False, it breaks the list in half with each test of one element.

5. False, in Fortran 77, the position within a character string is not a subscript. The declarations of such a list do not show a second subscript.

Part Two: Multiple Choice

1. d.

2. c is best.

3. a. Subscript bounds cannot be type real.

4. b. Answer e is tempting, but not true.

5. e. Method c is hopelessly inefficient for all but the smallest lists.

6. b.

7. c. If everything goes just wrong, one guess can leave 32 possibilities, two guesses 16 possibilities, ..., 6 guesses 1 possibility. However, that one possibility has not yet been guessed and that is the 7th guess that is needed in the worst case.

8. e. Choices a to d are nonsense or false.

9. d. is better than e because working on sorted lists is not unique to multi-level searches.

10. e. Both c and d are true.

Part Three: Syntax

1. This example is syntactically correct, although one should not deal harshly with a student who "corrects" the last subscript bound from 10 to 100. In the real world, the upper bound of 100 is more likely to be correct in context.

2. Correct. The declaration for NUMBER uses the abbreviated form with default lower subscript bound of 1.

3. Correct. (If you have a dialect of Fortran where this declaration is not accepted, you may want to allow your students to "correct" it to the nonstandard form your system accepts.)

4. Missing type, perhaps

        INTEGER LIST (-20 : 20), RESULT (-20 : 20)

5. If the "intent" is to have subscripts 2, 4, 6, 8, and 10 only, skipping all the odd numbers, this is impossible in Fortran.

Part Four: Output

1.

RUN ONE
    100
      64

```
        36
        16
         4
```

2.

```
RUN TWO
         3
         7
        13
        19
        29
```

3. a.

```
RUN THREE
INPUT DATA   LOOK:     5
```

4. b.

```
RUN THREE
INPUT DATA   LOOK:    15
FOUND:  3
```

5.

```
RUN FOUR
   85   44   33   17   12
```

6.

```
RUN FIVE
   3 7
   4 6
```

Part Five: Programming

1.

```
      PROGRAM SUM
C     READS AND ADDS TWO NUMBERS UP TO 101 DECIMAL DIGITS
      INTEGER DIGITA (0 : 100), DIGITB (0 : 100), DIGITC (0 : 100)
      INTEGER HIDIGA, HIDIGB, HIDIGC
      CALL READNR (DIGITA, HIDIGA)
      CALL READNR (DIGITB, HIDIGB)
      CALL ADD (DIGITA, HIDIGA, DIGITB, HIDIGB, DIGITC, HIDIGC)
C     PRINT SAME NUMBER OF DIGITS IN EACH NUMBER
      CALL PRINTD (DIGITA, HIDIGC)
      CALL PRINTD (DIGITB, HIDIGC)
      CALL PRNTLN (HIDIGC)
      CALL PRINTD (DIGITC, HIDIGC)
      END


      SUBROUTINE READNR (DIGIT, HIDIG)
C     READS A NUMBER, LOW ORDER DIGIT FIRST, STOPS ON -1 SIGNAL DIGIT
      INTEGER DIGIT (0 : 100), HIDIG, PLACE, BUFDIG
      CALL CLEAR (DIGIT, HIDIG)
      DO 28 PLACE = 0, 100
         READ *, BUFDIG
         IF (BUFDIG .EQ. -1) THEN
            GO TO 29
         ELSE
            DIGIT (PLACE) = BUFDIG
            HIDIG = PLACE
```

```
         END IF
   28 CONTINUE
   29 END


      SUBROUTINE CLEAR (DIGIT, HIDIG)
C     SETS A NUMBER TO ZERO
      INTEGER DIGIT (0 : 100), PLACE, HIDIG
      DO 18 PLACE = 0, 100
         DIGIT (PLACE) = 0
   18 CONTINUE
      HIDIG = 0
      END


      SUBROUTINE ADD (DIGITA, HIDIGA, DIGITB, HIDIGB, DIGITC, HIDIGC)
C     ADDS TWO NUMBERS WITH CARRIES FROM PLACE TO PLACE
      INTEGER DIGITA (0 : 100), DIGITB (0 : 100), DIGITC (0 : 100)
      INTEGER HIDIGA, HIDIGB, HIDIGC, PLACE, CARRY
      CALL CLEAR (DIGITC, HIDIGC)
      HIDIGC = MAX (HIDIGA, HIDIGB)
      CARRY = 0
      DO 18 PLACE = 0, HIDIGC
         DIGITC (PLACE) = DIGITA (PLACE) + DIGITB (PLACE) + CARRY
         IF (DIGITC (PLACE) .GT. 9) THEN
            DIGITC (PLACE) = DIGITC (PLACE) - 10
            CARRY = 1
         ELSE
            CARRY = 0
         END IF
   18 CONTINUE
      IF (CARRY .EQ. 1) THEN
C        CARRY INTO A NEW PLACE
         HIDIGC = HIDIGC + 1
         DIGITC (HIDIGC) = 1
      END IF
      END


      SUBROUTINE PRINTD (DIGIT, HIDIG)
C     PRINTS THE HIDIG + 1 LEAST SIGNIFICANT DIGITS OF A NUMBER
      INTEGER DIGIT (0 : 100), HIDIG, PLACE
      PRINT '(T11, 101I1)', (DIGIT (PLACE), PLACE = HIDIG, 0, -1)
      END


      SUBROUTINE PRNTLN (HIDIG)
C     PRINTS HIDIG + 1 DASHES TO FORM A LINE
      INTEGER HIDIG, PLACE
      PRINT '(T11, 101A1)', ('-', PLACE = HIDIG, 0, -1)
      END

RUN SUM
          1234567890123456789
          0002626262626262613
          -------------------
          1237194152749719402
```

2. For this problem, replace the subroutine ADD in the solution to Problem 1
    with the following subroutine MULT, and, of course, replace the call to
    ADD with a call to MULT.

```
      SUBROUTINE MULT (DIGITA, HIDIGA, DIGITB, HIDIGB, DIGITC, HIDIGC)
C     MULTIPLIES TWO LARGE INTEGERS
C     DOES NOT CHECK FOR OVERFLOW (I.E., PRODUCTS .GE. 10 ** 101)
      INTEGER DIGITA (0 : 100), DIGITB (0 : 100), DIGITC (0 : 100)
      INTEGER HIDIGA, HIDIGB, HIDIGC, PLACEA, PLACEB, PLACEC, CARRY
      CALL CLEAR (DIGITC, HIDIGC)
      HIDIGC = HIDIGA + HIDIGB
      DO 18 PLACEA = 0, HIDIGA
         DO 28 PLACEB = 0, HIDIGB
            DIGITC (PLACEA + PLACEB) = DIGITC (PLACEA + PLACEB) +
     +                                DIGITA (PLACEA) * DIGITB (PLACEB)
 28      CONTINUE
 18   CONTINUE
      DO 38 PLACEC = 0, HIDIGC
         IF (DIGITC (PLACEC) .GT. 9) THEN
            CARRY = DIGITC (PLACEC) / 10
            DIGITC (PLACEC) = MOD (DIGITC (PLACEC), 10)
            DIGITC (PLACEC + 1) = DIGITC (PLACEC + 1) + CARRY
         ELSE
            CARRY = 0
         END IF
 38   CONTINUE
      IF (CARRY .NE. 0) THEN
C        CARRY OUT OF THE HIDIGC PLACE
         HIDIGC = HIDIGC + 1
      END IF
      END
```

RUN PROD

```
                 0000000000000001234567890123456789
                 0000000000000000026262626262613
                 ----------------------------------
                 32422995094151226682056592717729657
```

FILES 7

This chapter is a brief but solid introduction to an extremely important topic, the permanent storage of data. Many computations are not just done, used, and forgotten. The results are saved in computer-readable form for future reference and to form the basis for future computations. Files are the computer's permanent and semi-permanent storage media.

How Much File Processing Is Really Necessary?

By the time this part of the book is reached, the end of the semester or quarter is making its presence felt, and the instructor may be wondering "What do my students absolutely have to know about files?" Our answer is a student must know how to handle sequential files.

There are several reasons for this answer. The first reason is for debugging programs that are not essentially file processing programs. By now, the programs are sufficiently complex that they do not work the first time they are put on the computer, so they require several debugging runs. Moreover, by now, the input data for the programs is more extensive than just a number or two. The student should not be retyping the input data for each debugging run. This means that the input data should be permanent, and therefore should be read from a file.

If you have interactive editing but batch execution, one of the best ways to debug is to put lots of debugging output statements in the program, directing the output to a file. Then the output file can be scanned selectively using the features of the editor.

A second reason why we think a student should be comfortable with sequential files at the end of the course is that sequential file processing resembles working with the standard input and output files so closely that there is little more to learn. On some systems, the student has been using files since the day the first program was run.

Main Memory and Auxiliary Memory

We needed terms to distinguish between the extremely high speed, high cost, "internal" memory of the computer and the relatively low speed, low cost "external" memory furnished by tapes, disks, and the like. Main memory is that part of the computer's information store that the central processing unit is in constant contact with during the course of the computation. Auxiliary memory is where the information gets dumped ("backed up" is more polite) when main memory is getting full.

Since the processing unit is not in constant contact with data in auxiliary memory, auxiliary memory devices can be slower, and in most cases cheaper than main memory. Some auxiliary memory media can be physically removed from the computer (tapes and removable disks). This adds another dimension to auxiliary memory—data security, permanence, and transportability to other computers.

Permanence

We stress the permanence aspect of information storage in auxiliary memory. Since the computer deals on a microsecond to microsecond basis with the information in main memory and the permanent copy of the information resides on a file in auxiliary memory. The most important concept in file processing is the passing of information from auxiliary memory to main memory and back to auxiliary memory.

When a file processing program starts, main memory contains garbage and auxiliary memory contains the most recent version of the file, written the last time the file was processed. Therefore main memory is initialized from auxiliary memory before any meaningful calculations can take place. Finally, all calculated results that are to be preserved must be written back to auxiliary memory before the program execution ends.

The Black Book System of Programs and Files

The black book system of programs illustrates this idea nicely. If you have time for just one file processing example, the black book example will do splendidly. The black book example is designed to sidestep the more delicate questions about which pieces of information to have available in main memory at which stage of the calculations. *All* of the information is read into main memory before any of the calculations are done, and *all* the information is written to auxiliary memory at the conclusion of the execution. Assuming it all fits in main memory, this method makes for the simplest programs to process the file.

Directly Accessed Files

The payroll system of programs and files is a "real" application. It remembers hourly pay rates and year-to-date totals from week to week. It provides a large data base both for the payroll functions and for management inquiry systems. The payroll system of programs that generates all of our paychecks is probably little different from this example in principle. It just has more of the same kinds of details.

If many of your students are going to be taking a data base management course, this example is an excellent introduction. If they are not going to be taking a data base course, they need this example even more. Truthfully, however, because of its complexity and lateness in the semester, this topic is often omitted.

We miss it because of the insight it has to offer about how so many programs you will encounter are organized. Sooner or later, the student should learn about indexes and not moving data around in slow speed memory. But there are always other courses to take after this one!

Vocabulary

auxiliary memory
CLOSE statement
creating a file
data base
direct file access
end-of-file
END option
file peek program
file dump program
index file to a directly accessed file
magnetic disk
magnetic tape
main memory
OPEN statement
parity check
READ statement
record number
REWIND statement
sequential file access
system of programs
system of subprograms
tape drive
unit number
updating a file
virtual memory
WRITE statement

Chapter Outline

Examination Questions

Part One: True or False

Indicate which of the sentences below are true and which are false. If a sentence is false, explain what is wrong.

1.   A unit number is the name by which a file is listed in the system directory.

2.   A typical disk drive can transmit data at a much faster rate than a typical tape drive.

3.   The phrase, "random access" means that you do not know where your data is being stored on disk.

4.   If 100 records are stored on a disk in a direct access file, it will take almost exactly the same time to read all 100 records, no matter what order they are read.

5.   If every record of a file must be read and processed during the execution of a program, then direct file access usually offers no significant time advantage over sequential file access.

Part Two: Multiple Choice

Choose one best answer.

1.   Reasons for storing data on disk are

   a.   to save it permanently or semipermanently
   b.   to conserve space in main memory.
   c.   to make it available to several programs and users.
   d.   to provide for much larger files than can possibly fit in main memory.
   e.   all of the above.

2.   The sequence of steps in updating a record of an auxiliary memory file is

   a.   locating the record, changing the record, and writing the record.
   b.   reading the record, writing the record, and changing the record.
   c.   locating the record, writing the record, changing the record, and rereading the changed record.
   d.   locating the record, changing the record, reading the record, and rewriting the record.
   e.   locating the record, reading the record, changing the record, and rewriting the record.

3.   The STATUS option in an OPEN statement tells

   a.   whether the file is to be directly or sequentially accessed.
   b.   whether the file has any data errors or bad sectors.
   c.   whether the operating system should expect the file name to already be in its directory.
   d.   whether the file is currently in use by another program.
   e.   whether the file has been updated within the preceding 24 hour period.

4.

   a.   replaces the END statement at the end of a subroutine that reads from a file.
   b.   makes the END statement at the end of the current subprogram optional.
   c.   specifies the label of the last statement in the program.
   d.   specifies the label of the statement to be executed if an end-of-file condition is detected which reading the file.

    e.   specifies the data value that is to be recognized as a termination signal when data is read from the file.

5.

    a.   can only be used with tape files, not disk files.

    b.   closes the file.

    c.   positions a file at its beginning.

    d.   must precede all reading from or writing to a file.

    e.   erases the entire contents of the file.

Part Three: Syntax

Indicate which of the following Fortran statements are syntactically correct, and which are not. If a statement is not correct, rewrite it to make it correct, or indicate why this is not possible. Be sure not to change the "intent" of the statement in the process of correcting the syntax. Assume all variables are correctly declared.

1.

```
WRITE (11, *) A, B, C
```

2.

```
WRITE (11, 12) A, B, C
```

3.

```
READ (UNIT = 5), X, Y, Z
```

4.

```
OPEN (UNIT = '1', FILE = 'MYFILE', ACCESS = 'DIRECT', RECL = '20')
```

5.

```
WRITE (UNIT = '1', RECL = '12') NEWREC
```

6.

```
READ (UNIT = 2, FILE = MYFILE, ACCESS = SEQUENTIAL, END = 19), X, Y, Z
```

7.

```
READ (5, *) X
```

8.

```
CLOSE (UNIT 12)
```

9.

```
WRITE (6, '(3F10.5)') (A (I), I = 1, 3)
```

10.

```
WRITE (UNIT = 6, FMT = '(A)', END = 999) 'END OF RUN'
```

Part Four: Calculation

Perform the indicated calculations and give the answers. Show all work.

1. A floppy disk rotates at 300 revolutions per minute. In one standard format, each disk track has 9 sectors with 512 bytes of data stored per sector. Once the read head has been properly positioned over the correct track and sector, what is the rate at which data can be transmitted from this floppy disk drive to a computer. Express the answer in bytes per second.

2. The floppy disk described in Problem 1 has 40 tracks per side and can record data on both sides of the disk. What is the maximum capacity of the floppy disk in bytes. (One byte is approximately one ASCII or EBCDIC character.)

Part Five: Programming

1.   The Problem: Write two related programs, to be run in sequence. The first program should read up to 20 names from the standard input file, (interactive input with prompts is preferable if your system supports it), sorts the names into alphabetic order, and writes the sorted list to a permanent file. The second program (a separately executed main program and not a second subroutine) should read the sorted list from the file and print the names in order on the printer. It is important that in neither program, the user specifies the number of names, except implicitly by typing a specific number of input names before typing the termination signal. Sample Output:

```
RUN FIRST
ENTER A NAME (LAST NAME, FIRST NAME) OR THE SIGNAL 'NO MORE NAMES'
CARLYLE, THOMAS
ENTER A NAME (LAST NAME, FIRST NAME) OR THE SIGNAL 'NO MORE NAMES'
WELSH, JANE
ENTER A NAME (LAST NAME, FIRST NAME) OR THE SIGNAL 'NO MORE NAMES'
RUSKIN, JOHN
ENTER A NAME (LAST NAME, FIRST NAME) OR THE SIGNAL 'NO MORE NAMES'
GRAY, EFFIE
ENTER A NAME (LAST NAME, FIRST NAME) OR THE SIGNAL 'NO MORE NAMES'
NO MORE NAMES
```

(All subsequent output is written to a permanent disk file.)

```
RUN SECOND

THE LIST OF NAMES IS AS FOLLOWS:

CARLYLE, THOMAS
GRAY, EFFIE
RUSKIN, JOHN
WELSH, JANE
```

Answer Key

Part One: True or False

1. False, it is the number by which the file is referenced within a Fortran program.

2. False, the data transmission rates are approximately equal. It is the latency or delay time in locating a particular record that differs between the two kinds of devices.

3. False, it means that the records of the file can be accessed in any order without appreciable time penalty.

4. False is the better answer. There is a workably small upper limit on the total access time that is never exceeded for any permutation of the 100 record accesses. However, if the records are accessed in an order that minimizes the head movement from track to track and minimizes the latency wait time for the desired information on a track to pass under the read/write head, the total access time can be reduced substantially, often by an order of magnitude.

5. True. A possible exception is when two differently ordered sequential files need to be synchronized for processing. In that case, (not treated in the book), sequential access is decidedly inferior to direct access.

Part Two: Multiple Choice

1. e. all of the above.

2. e.

3. he values of the STATUS option treated in this chapter are STATUS = 'OLD' and STATUS = 'NEW'

4. d.

5. c. all of the others are false.

Part Three: Syntax

1.
```
     WRITE (11, *) A, B, C              <--correct syntax
```

2.
```
     WRITE (11, 12) A, B, C            <--correct syntax, 12 is the label of a
                                       <--FORMAT statement
```

3.
```
     READ (UNIT = 5, FMT = '(3I8)') X, Y, Z
                                  <--missing format specification and
                                  <--extra comma
```

4.
```
     OPEN (UNIT = 1, FILE = 'MYFILE', ACCESS = 'DIRECT', RECL = 20)
                                  <--too many options enquoted
```

5.
```
     WRITE (UNIT = 1, REC = 12) NEWREC
                                  <--format specification is not required
                                  <--because the default for directly
                                  <--accessed files is unformatted
```

6.

```
      READ (UNIT = 2, FILE = 'MYFILE', END = 19) X, Y, Z
                                  <--ACCESS option deleted, comma deleted
                                  <--enquoted FILE name
```

7.

```
      READ (5, *) X                     <--correct
```

8.

```
      CLOSE (UNIT = 12)                 <--almost correct
```

9.

```
      WRITE (6, '(3F10.5)') (A (I), I = 1, 3)
                                        <--correct
```

10.

```
      WRITE (UNIT = 6, FMT = '(A)') 'END OF RUN'
                                    <--the END option is only in READ
                                    <--statements
```

Part Four: Calculation

1. 300 rev/min × 1/60 min/sec × 9 sectors/rev × 512 bytes/sector = 23,040 bytes/sec

2. 40 tracks/side × 2 sides/disk × 9 sectors/track × 512 bytes/sector = 368,640 bytes/disk

Part Five: Programming

1.

```
      PROGRAM FIRST
C     ACCEPTS NAMES, SORTS THEM, AND WRITES THEM TO A FILE
      INTEGER MAXNAM, NRNAME, NAMLEN
      PARAMETER (MAXNAM = 20, NAMLEN = 25)
      CHARACTER NAME (1 : MAXNAM) * (NAMLEN)
      CALL RDNAME (NAME, MAXNAM, NRNAME)
      CALL SORTNM (NAME, NRNAME)
      CALL WRFILE (NAME, NRNAME)
      END

      SUBROUTINE RDNAME (NAME, MAXNAM, NRNAME)
C     READS A LIST OF NAMES, TERMINATING ON THE SIGNAL 'NO MORE NAMES'
      INTEGER MAXNAM, NAMLEN, N
      PARAMETER (NAMLEN = 25)
      CHARACTER SIGNAL * (NAMLEN)
      PARAMETER (SIGNAL = 'NO MORE NAMES')
      CHARACTER NAME (1 : MAXNAM) * (NAMLEN), BUFFER * (NAMLEN)
      NRNAME = 0
      DO 18 N = 1, MAXNAM
         PRINT *, 'ENTER A NAME (LAST NAME, FIRST NAME)',
     +           'OR THE SIGNAL ''NO MORE NAMES'''
         READ *, BUFFER
         IF (BUFFER .NE. SIGNAL) THEN
            NAME (N) = BUFFER
            NRNAME = N
         ELSE
            GO TO 19
```

```
           END IF
    18 CONTINUE
    19 END


       SUBROUTINE SORTNM (NAME, NRNAME)
C      SORTS A SHORT LIST OF NAMES
       INTEGER NRNAME, I, J, NAMLEN
       PARAMETER (NAMLEN = 25)
       CHARACTER NAME (1 : NRNAME) * (NAMLEN), TEMP * (NAMLEN)
       DO 18 I = 1, NRNAME - 1
          DO 28 J = I+1, NRNAME
             IF (NAME (I) .GT. NAME (J)) THEN
C               SWAP THEM INTO THE CORRECT ORDER
                TEMP = NAME (I)
                NAME (I) = NAME (J)
                NAME (J) = TEMP
             END IF
    28    CONTINUE
    18 CONTINUE
       END


       SUBROUTINE WRFILE (NAME, NRNAME)
C      WRITES A LIST OF NAMES TO A FILE
       INTEGER NRNAME, NAMLEN, N
       PARAMETER (NAMLEN = 25)
       CHARACTER NAME (1 : NRNAME) * (NAMLEN)
       OPEN (UNIT = 1, FILE = 'NAMFIL')
       REWIND (UNIT = 1)
       DO 18 N = 1, NRNAME
          WRITE (UNIT = 1, FMT = '(A25)') NAME (N)
    18 CONTINUE
       END



       PROGRAM SECOND
C      REREADS THE FILE WRITTEN BY THE PROGRAM FIRST AND PRINTS THE LIST
       INTEGER MAXNAM, NRNAME, NAMLEN
       PARAMETER (MAXNAM = 20, NAMLEN = 25)
       CHARACTER NAME (1 : MAXNAM) * (NAMLEN)
       CALL RDFILE (NAME, MAXNAM, NRNAME)
       CALL PRLIST (NAME, NRNAME)
       END


       SUBROUTINE RDFILE (NAME, MAXNAM, NRNAME)
C      READS NAMES FROM A FILE, STOPPING ON END-OF-FILE
       INTEGER MAXNAM, NRNAME, NAMLEN, N
       PARAMETER (NAMLEN = 25)
       CHARACTER NAME (1 : MAXNAM) * (NAMLEN)
       OPEN (UNIT = 1, FILE = 'NAMFIL', STATUS = 'OLD')
       DO 18 N = 1, MAXNAM
          READ (UNIT = 1, FMT = '(A25)', END = 19) NAME (N)
          NRNAME = N
    18 CONTINUE
    19 END
```

```
      SUBROUTINE PRLIST (NAME, NRNAME)
C     PRINTS A LIST OF NAMES
      INTEGER NRNAME, NAMLEN, N
      PARAMETER (NAMLEN = 25)
      CHARACTER NAME (1 : NRNAME) * (NAMLEN)
      PRINT *, 'THE LIST OF NAMES IS AS FOLLOWS:'
      PRINT *
      DO 18 N = 1, NRNAME
         PRINT *, NAME (N)
   18 CONTINUE
      END
```

2. The program that reads the existing file and appends additional names to it is essentially a synthesis of the two programs FIRST and SECOND, with minor changes made in the main program (now named THIRD) and in the subroutine RDNAME, which now must assume a not necessarily zero starting value for its dummy argument NRNAME, the count of the actual number of names in the list.

```
      PROGRAM THIRD
C     REREADS THE FILE WRITTEN BY THE PROGRAM FIRST, ACCEPTS NEW NAMES,
C     AND REWRITES THE FILE
      INTEGER MAXNAM, NRNAME, NAMLEN
      PARAMETER (MAXNAM = 20, NAMLEN = 25)
      CHARACTER NAME (1 : MAXNAM) * (NAMLEN)
      CALL RDFILE (NAME, MAXNAM, NRNAME)
      CALL RDNAME (NAME, MAXNAM, NRNAME)
      CALL SORTNM (NAME, NRNAME)
      CALL WRFILE (NAME, NRNAME)
      END


      SUBROUTINE RDFILE (NAME, MAXNAM, NRNAME)
C     READS NAMES FROM A FILE, STOPPING ON END-OF-FILE
      INTEGER MAXNAM, NRNAME, NAMLEN, N
      PARAMETER (NAMLEN = 25)
      CHARACTER NAME (1 : MAXNAM) * (NAMLEN)
      OPEN (UNIT = 1, FILE = 'NAMFIL', STATUS = 'OLD')
      DO 18 N = 1, MAXNAM
         READ (UNIT = 1, FMT = '(A25)', END = 19) NAME (N)
         NRNAME = N
   18 CONTINUE
   19 END


      SUBROUTINE RDNAME (NAME, MAXNAM, NRNAME)
C     READS ADDITIONAL NAMES, TERMINATING ON THE SIGNAL 'NO MORE NAMES'
      INTEGER MAXNAM, NAMLEN, N
      PARAMETER (NAMLEN = 25)
      CHARACTER SIGNAL * (NAMLEN)
      PARAMETER (SIGNAL = 'NO MORE NAMES')
      CHARACTER NAME (1 : MAXNAM) * (NAMLEN), BUFFER * (NAMLEN)
      DO 18 N = NRNAME + 1, MAXNAM
         PRINT *, 'ENTER A NAME (LAST NAME, FIRST NAME)',
     +            'OR THE SIGNAL ''NO MORE NAMES'''
         READ *, BUFFER
         IF (BUFFER .NE. SIGNAL) THEN
            NAME (N) = BUFFER
            NRNAME = N
```

```
          ELSE
              GO TO 19
          END IF
   18 CONTINUE
   19 END


      SUBROUTINE SORTNM (NAME, NRNAME)
C     SORTS A SHORT LIST OF NAMES
      INTEGER NRNAME, I, J, NAMLEN
      PARAMETER (NAMLEN = 25)
      CHARACTER NAME (1 : NRNAME) * (NAMLEN), TEMP * (NAMLEN)
      DO 18 I = 1, NRNAME - 1
         DO 28 J = I + 1, NRNAME
            IF (NAME (I) .GT. NAME (J)) THEN
C               SWAP THEM INTO THE CORRECT ORDER
                TEMP = NAME (I)
                NAME (I) = NAME (J)
                NAME (J) = TEMP
            END IF
   28    CONTINUE
   18 CONTINUE
      END


      SUBROUTINE WRFILE (NAME, NRNAME)
C     WRITES A LIST OF NAMES TO A FILE
      INTEGER NRNAME, NAMLEN, N
      PARAMETER (NAMLEN = 25)
      CHARACTER NAME (1 : NRNAME) * (NAMLEN)
      OPEN (UNIT = 1, FILE = 'NAMFIL')
      REWIND (UNIT = 1)
      DO 18 N = 1, NRNAME
         WRITE (UNIT = 1, FMT = '(A25)') NAME (N)
   18 CONTINUE
      END
```

CHARACTER DATA 8

With Chapter 8, we reach the "optional" part of the book. There are still syntactic features to be introduced and programming techniques to learn, but the core of programming syntax and methodology is already in place.

The Importance of Character Processing

The importance of character string processing is less than obvious to many scientific programmers and to students with strong science and engineering backgrounds. True they are very useful in identifying the parts of you numerical output, but in a pinch many scientific programmers believe that they could do without them.

Except in narrowly circumscribed areas of numerical calculation, this is far from a true picture of the world of computer science. Most programming is nonnumerical. Not only is "business" computer programming concerned with names, dates, descriptions, titles, and other nonnumeric quantities; scientific programming is also concerned with character strings.

Amino acid chains are represented as sequences of letters. Pattern recognition is a central goal in artificial intelligence and robotics research. The central problems in computer programs for particle physics are not computing the trajectories but coping with the enormous quantity of data generated by the experiments.

Word Processing

Moreover, computer scientists earn their living (at least some of them) by writing useful programs. One such extremely useful program, treated at length in this chapter, is word processing. We expect that however much a computer scientist or other knowledgeable person professes to need a "personal" or microcomputer for the purposes of writing and running programs, when the microcomputer finally arrives and settles into its permanent place in the working environment, it will be used most often not for running programs, but for word processing.

Once you use a word processor, even a lousy one, you will never go back to a typewriter. You can always correct your work cleanly on a word processor, but it has always been a trial and a tribulation to correct your work on a typewriter. You may not decide to write your own word processor, although there is immense satisfaction in using a production program of your own devising, but having an idea of how word processors work can help you get the most out of someone else's word processor, and to get a sense of why some unfulfilled demands placed on word processors are essentially unfulfillable (in reasonable time and space).

Aside of the fact that word processing deals with character data, its basic methods are the bread and butter of computer science: lists, searching, insertion, deletion, creating, updating, and saving files, handling variable length data, etc. Word processing presents all the old algorithms in a new setting.

Elegant Touches

In many applications, character constants are adequate, but character variables and the character string manipulation techniques in this chapter can provide elegant extras. File names and headings can be generated during execution, rather than being fixed when the program is written. A program that reads and updates a file named "XXX.17" can decompose the file name into the title "XXX" and the sequence number, 17, increment the sequence number to 18, and reunite the two parts to write the updated version of the file as "XXX.18". These fine touches are not really frills, although their absence can be forgiven in programs written by beginners or under time pressure. These niceties are what make one program user friendly and another program an abomination to use.

Purely For Fun and Practice

The text analysis programs in Section 8.3 probably serve no useful purpose other than practice in the techniques of computer programming, although each of these applications was once thought to have promise. Their major problem is that they measure the characteristics of a text too superficially. The programming techniques are available to measure more intricate statistics, but the applications people have little idea what statistics would be meaningful or enlightening.

Palindromes and alliteration are purely for fun, at least until some biochemist proves an assertion of the sort that certain proteins are neurotransmitter receptors if and only if their amino acid sequences are palindromes. (That's not true, but it sounds as if it could be.)

Faults of Fortran

No computer language is perfect. Even the "new" Fortran 77 standards don't go far enough in certain areas. Previous Fortran standards did not even include character data type so the current standards are a big improvement, but they fall short of the flexible and convenient character data type of, say, BASIC, which has been around to emulate for quite a while.

Fortran character strings are still fixed length, although the automatic padding with blanks and truncation conventions of Fortran make Fortran character strings a pleasure compared to the character data type in standard Pascal. (You can't even compare or assign to standard Pascal character strings of unequal length.)

The length function, LEN, is useless except for dummy arguments of a subprogram, because the length is almost always the declared length. The concatenation operator is almost unusable, and the restrictions on substring assignment make it difficult to use.

Applause for Fortran

On the positive side, the Fortran notation for substrings listing starting and stopping positions is very easy to use and very understandable. The built-in function INDEX is extremely useful and convenient.

The ability to use character variables for formats permits calculated output formats, a very advanced feature. For example, it is possible to have the width of a field in an output line depend on the size of the number to be printed.

The point of this criticism and praise is not that we know how to design the world's best programming language and that Fortran is or isn't close to our ideal. The point is that even beginning students should be encouraged to think critically and not to accept on faith that because a committee of experts decided on the current Fortran 77 standard, it is a perfect language. The continuing work of one of us (Brainerd) on the Fortran standards committee is partly to see if the language can't be made even better.

Vocabulary

CHAR built-in function
character assignment
character constant
character parameter
character string
character variable
concatenation
dummy argument declaration
ICHAR built-in function
INDEX built-in function
LEN built-in function
length of a character string
pattern matching ("find" editing command)
substring
substring assignment
text editing
trimmed length of a character string
word processing

Chapter Outline

Examination Questions

Part One: True or False

Indicate which of the sentences below are true and which are false. If a sentence is false, explain what is wrong.

1. The built-in function ICHAR converts a character string from fixed to variable length.

2. In Fortran, a substring cannot have length zero.

3. It does not matter whether a computer uses the ASCII character set or the EBCDIC character set when the character strings to be compared consist only of uppercase letters.

4. The length of a character variable depends on the value assigned to it.

5. A substring cannot exceed in length the string from which it is extracted.

Part Two: Multiple Choice

1. Character strings in an input file

    a. are always surrounded by apostrophes.
    b. are never surrounded by apostrophes.
    c. have a length determined by the length declaration of the variables into which they are read.
    d. must be surrounded by apostrophes if the default format is used.
    e. must not be surrounded by apostrophes if the default format is used.

2. 2. In a substring reference STR (K : L)

    a. K must be less than or equal to L.
    b. K must be greater than zero.
    c. L must be less than or equal to the declared length of STR.
    d. L must be less than or equal to the trimmed length of STR.
    e. a, b, and c above.

3. In a list of character strings declared CHARACTER WORD (1 : 100) * 15, the correct way to reference the seventh character of the fifteenth word is

    a. WORD (7, 15)
    b. WORD (7 : 15)
    c. WORD (15 : 7)
    d. WORD (15) (7)
    e. WORD (15) (7 : 7)

4. The built-in function INDEX

    a. ignores trailing blanks in the search string.
    b. requires its two arguments to be the same declared length.
    c. does not work (i.e., reports an error condition and stops) if there are two or more instances of the search string as a substring of the other string.
    d. does not work (i.e., reports an error condition and stops) if there are no instances of the search string as a substring of the other string.
    e. will not report a match if one string has trailing blanks while the other string does not.

5. The declaration CHARACTER GLUNK *(*)

    a. means that GLUNK is a character string of variable length.
    b. means that GLUNK takes on the system default for character string length.

c. means that GLUNK is an array of character strings with subscript bounds declared in the main program.

d. means that GLUNK is a character valued dummy argument whose length agrees with that of the corresponding actual (supplied) argument.

e. means that GLUNK is a character valued dummy argument whose length is also a dummy argument.

Part Three: Fill In

Write the word, phrase, or expression that best completes the following sentences.

1. If A = '123' and B = '456' then the value of A // B is _____.

2. If A = 'THERE ARE FEW TESTABLE FEATURES IN CHAPTER 8', and B = ' ', then the value of INDEX (A, B) is _____.

3. If A = 'ANY OLD CHARACTER STRING', B = 'ANY', and C = 'OLD', then the value of A (INDEX (A, B) : INDEX (A, C)) is _____.

4. If X = '$', then the value of CHAR (ICHAR (X)) is _____ when the computer uses _____ character set.

5. When the character strings 'WARPLE' and 'WARPLE   ' are compared, the result of the comparison is _____.

Part Four: Output

What output will be printed when the following programs are run?

1.
```
   PROGRAM ONE
   CHARACTER A * 20
   INTEGER N
   A = 'A SEPARATE MATTER'
   DO 18 N = INDEX (A, 'RAT'), LEN (A)
      PRINT *, A(N : N)
18 CONTINUE
   END
```

2.
```
   PROGRAM TWO
   CHARACTER A * 20
   INTEGER N
   A = 'A MATTER OF SMALL INDIFFERENCE AND CONSTERNATION'
   PRINT *, A
   PRINT *, A (3 : 5)
   END
```

3.
```
   PROGRAM THREE
   CHARACTER A * 20
   INTEGER N
   A = 'MATTER IS ENERGY'
   PRINT '(21A1)', (A (N : N), N = 1, LEN (A)), '!'
   END
```

4.

```
     PROGRAM FOUR
     CHARACTER A * 20
     INTEGER N
     A = 'ABCDEFGHIJKLMNOPQRSTUVWXYZ'
     DO 18 N = 1, LEN (A)
        PRINT *, ICHAR (A (N : N)) - ICHAR ('A')
  18 CONTINUE
     END
```

5.

```
     PROGRAM FIVE
     CHARACTER A * 20
     INTEGER N
     A = 'ASTHMA'
     DO 18 N = 1, 6
        IF (A (N : N) .LE. A (7-N : 7-N)) THEN
           PRINT *, A (N : N)
        END IF
  18 CONTINUE
     END
```

Part Five: Programming

1. The Problem: There is a famous rhymed spelling rule about "i" before
   "e", except after "c" or when sounded like "a" as in "neighbor" and
   "weigh". Write a program to read a list of words (15 characters maximum
   length) and to see if the word has either the letter pair "ie" or the letter
   pair "ei". If the word has the "i" before the "e", then the word should
   be listed starting in column 11 and an "X" should be placed in column 31
   of that line. If the word has an "e" before the "i", then the word should
   be listed starting in column 11 and an "X" should be placed in column 41
   of that line. If a word contains neither "ie" nor "ei", then the word
   should not be listed at all. Place appropriate headings on the top line of
   output. Input Data:

```
RELIEF
RECEIVE
PROCEED
LIE
LYE
RELY
NEIGHBOR
HEIGHT
WEIGHT
CLIENT
QUIET
QUIT
```

   Sample Output:

```
RUN IETEST


          WORD                 IE        EI


          RELIEF               X
          RECEIVE                        X
          LIE                  X
```

```
NEIGHBOR                    X
HEIGHT                      X
WEIGHT                      X
CLIENT          X
QUIET           X
```

Answer Key

Part One: True or False

1. False, it converts from type character to type integer.
2. True.
3. True.
4. False, it is fixed by its declaration.
5. True.

Part Two: Multiple Choice

1. d is best.
2. e because d is not correct.
3. e.
4. e.
5. d.

Part Three: Fill In

1. '123456'
2. 6
3. 'ANY O'
4. '$'; either the ASCII or the EBCDID or any other Note: the character set must contain the character '$'
5. equality, 'WARPLE' .EQ. 'WARPLE   '

Part Four: Output

1.
```
RUN ONE
R
A
T
E

M
A
T
T
E
R
          <--blank line
          <--blank line
          <--blank line
```
2.
```
RUN TWO
A MATTER OF SMALL IN
MAT
```
3.
```
RUN THREE
MATTER IS ENERGY     !
```

4.

RUN FOUR
        0
        1
        2
        3
        4
        5
        6
        7
        8
        9
       10
       11
       12
       13
       14
       15
       16
       17
       18
       19

5.

RUN FIVE
A
H
M
A

Part Five: Programming

1.

```
      PROGRAM IETEST
C     DISPLAY EXAMPLES OF THE SPELLING RULE ON IE AND EI
      CHARACTER WORD * 15, SIGNAL * 15
      INTEGER COUNT, MANY
      PARAMETER (MANY = 10000,
     +           SIGNAL = 'QUIT')
      PRINT '(T11, A15, T31, A2, T41, A2)', 'WORD', 'IE', 'EI'
      PRINT *
      DO 18 COUNT = 1, MANY
         READ '(A15)', WORD
         IF (WORD .EQ. SIGNAL) THEN
            GO TO 19
         END IF
         IF (INDEX (WORD, 'IE') .NE. 0) THEN
            PRINT '(T11, A15, T31, A1)', WORD, 'X'
         ELSE IF (INDEX (WORD ,'EI') .NE. 0) THEN
            PRINT '(T11, A15, T41, A1)', WORD, 'X'
         END IF
   18 CONTINUE
   19 END
```

```
RUN IETEST

        WORD            IE      EI

        RELIEF          X
        RECEIVE                 X
        LIE             X
        NEIGHBOR                X
        HEIGHT                  X
        WEIGHT                  X
        CLIENT          X
        QUIET           X
```

MULTI-DIMENSIONAL ARRAYS 9

There really isn't much to say about the syntax of multi-dimensional arrays (assuming of course that one-dimensional arrays are already understood), and Figure 9.1 says it all.

Two-Dimensional Arrays

Locating an element in a two-dimensional array is like locating a point on usual cartesian graph paper, or locating a city by its latitude and longitude. Many cities have grids of avenues and streets that serve as convenient examples.

The telephone rate table, although not geometrical, is an example of a table in which the appropriate entry is located on the basis of two independent (orthoginal) determiners: the city called and the time of day. Neither alone is sufficient to specify the applicable rate, but both together uniquely determine the rate.

Three-Dimensional Arrays

Later in the chapter, a third variable, the city of origin is introduced. Figure 9.6 now shows the situation. The entries may now be visualized as occupying cubbyholes in a rectangular solid. Unless your students' geometric intuition is very good, it may be simpler just to say, "the appropriate rate is uniquely specified by three numbers, the city of origin code, the city of destination code, and the time of day code." Certainly, when there are four or more subscripts, the geometry will only confuse.

Nested Loops

When every element of a two-dimensional array must be processed, it is inevitable that the program takes the form of two nested DO blocks. Expressed in pseudocode, the algorithm has the general form

```
For every ROW
    For every COLUMN
        Process the value in ARRAY (ROW, COLUMN)
    Next COLUMN
Next ROW
```

Calculating a multiplication table shows this structure in a nutshell.

```
   DO 18 ROW = 1, 10
      DO 28 COL = 1, 10
         MTABLE (ROW, COL) = ROW * COL
28    CONTINUE
18 CONTINUE
```

Digital Graphics

The French impressionist painters long ago proved that you can create a picture out of discrete dots, and the television set reproves it daily. TV type display tubes and dot matrix printers are nothing but dot generators on a rectangular grid. Character display devices such a line printers can also be considered as grid dot generators if the size of each grid point is the size of, say, a printed asterisk (*).

The difference between high resolution graphics images and low resolution graphics images is how far away from the image you must be before you cease to see it as a collection of discrete dots and begin to see it as a complete picture. Fortunately, the same processing techniques apply to both high and low resolution graphics, so the programs in this chapter can be used regardless of which hardware you have.

The Data Acquisition Bottleneck

If you are lucky enough to have access to a video digitizer or "frame grabber", getting good input data to the image processing programs is no problem. For the rest of us, simulated video digitizer output is gained by the sweat of our brow (or of our lab assistant's brow in some cases). The simplest technique is to place a piece of semitransparent graph paper over a picture and to digitize the pixels by "eyeball". This is not very elegant, but it is effective.

For your information, the crater on Deimos was on the cover of Scientific American, and the origin of the following digital intensity data will be clear when its image is printed.

```
3 3 3 3 3 3 3 3 9 9 9 9 9 3 3 3 3 3 3 3 3 3 3 3
3 3 3 3 3 3 9 9 9 9 9 9 9 3 3 3 3 3 3 3 3 3 3 3
3 3 3 3 3 3 9 9 9 9 9 9 9 3 3 3 3 3 3 3 3 3 3 3
3 3 9 9 9 9 3 3 9 9 9 9 9 0 0 3 3 3 3 3 3 3 3 3
3 9 9 9 9 9 9 9 9 9 9 0 0 0 0 0 3 3 3 3 3 3 3 3
9 9 9 9 9 9 9 0 0 0 9 0 0 0 9 0 9 3 3 3 3 3 3 3
3 9 9 9 9 9 0 0 0 0 0 0 0 0 0 9 0 9 3 3 3 3 3 3
3 3 3 3 3 3 0 0 0 0 0 0 0 0 0 9 0 9 0 0 9 9 3 3
3 3 3 3 3 3 3 0 0 0 9 0 0 0 0 0 0 0 0 9 9 3 3 3
3 3 3 3 3 3 3 3 3 0 6 9 0 0 0 0 0 0 0 0 3 3 3 3
3 3 3 3 3 3 3 9 9 9 6 6 9 0 9 0 0 0 0 3 3 3 3 3
```

If you know what the image is, you can almost see it from the raw data display.

Image Enhancement

The quite remarkable thing about digital images is how good an image you can produce with how bad a collection of input data. For a start, bigger is better. Instead of one dot per pixel, print a "square" of 5 × 5 dots for each pixel. You will be surprised at how much better it makes the picture look.

Halftoning on a dot matrix printer or on a microcomputer graphics display screen does wonders for the apparent resolution of the picture. Display screens are partiularly good because they get very dark blacks (no dots) and very bright whites (or greens). In contrast, a printer image is very flat, ranging from the pure white of the paper to a light gray for the darkest printed character viewed from a sufficient distance that only the overall density and not the individual characters is visible.

If your students like this topic, they can have a ball doing research into methods of improving a digital image. Averaging nearby pixels, either before or after expanding each pixel to a larger size, has the effect of throwing the image slightly out of focus, thereby smoothing the rough staircase effect of diagonal lines in a digital image.

Interpolating values for intermediate points is now done by some large screen television sets to increase the apparent resolution. Compensations for permanent and transitory defects of the imaging system are now routinely applied to digitally transmitted images.

Function Graphs

The chief difficulty in learning to plot the graph of a function is in the scaling of a range of "world coordinates" in the x and y of the mathematical problem to a range of "screen or print coordinates" given by row and column number. The mathematically inclined will find this very easy, but the mathematically disinclined may find it very difficult.

If you use an overhead projector, a series of overlays are helpful. First make a base transparancy with the screen or printer coordinates of your computer display system. Then overlay it with a transparancy showing the mathematical x, y "world coordinates". The row number for the x axis and the column number for the y axis can not be clearly seen. Then on a third overlay, the distances involved in the scaling proportion can be drawn and labelled. Finally, the proportions can be solved for the screen coordinates as a function of the world coordinates, and vice versa.

Of course, the more points you plot, the better the graph looks. (See Figure 9.4 done on a microcomputer.) With functions, you do not have the problem of insufficient data, only of insufficient resolution. If you use a printer, make your graph the full size of a page, 55-60 lines by 132 columns, or of several pages if you draw it sideways.

Infinite Series Approximations to Functions

If your students have taken enough calculus to know about trigonometric functions and infinite series, the following project is meaningful. On the same set of axes, plot the functions

1. $y = \sin(x)$
2. $y = x$
3. $y = x - x^3/3!$
4. $y = x - x^3/3! + x^5/5!$
5. $y = x - x^3/3! + x^5/5! - x^7/7!$

As progressively more terms in the infinite series are included, the student can see the functions approximating $y = \sin(x)$ better and better over larger and larger intervals.

Vocabulary

cathode ray tube (CRT)
column number
COMMON statement
COMMON block
contrast enhancement
digital computer graphic
digital image
graph
gray scale
halftone
histogram
image acquisition
image enhancement
multi-dimensional array
pixel
printer graphic
row number
superposition
table
three-dimensional array
two-dimensional array
video digitizer
visual image processing

Chapter Outline

Examination Questions

Part One: True or False

Indicate which of the sentences below are true and which are false. If a sentence is false, explain what is wrong.

1. A two-dimensional array needs two subscripts to specify which element of the array is being referenced.

2. Superposition means building a complex picture out of simpler shapes.

3. A halftone is an image brightness half way between two of the ten digitized intensities, an image intensity, say, of 5.5.

4. A histogram is a bar graph where the height of each bar is proprotional to the data value for that category.

5. To plot the graph of a function for ranges of x and y values that include some negative values, you must use negative subscripts in the graph plotting array.

Part Two: Multiple Choice

Choose one BEST answer.

1. Five-dimensional arrays are
    a. permitted in Fortran.
    b. meaningless since there are only three dimensions in the real world.
    c. theoretically possible, but only implemented in other computer programming languages.
    d. limited to type integer.
    e. none of the above.

2. Superposition
    a. is not possible if the output device is a dot matrix printer.
    b. is possible only if the entire image is stored in computer memory before the image is printed.
    c. always results in a darker image.
    d. all of the above.
    e. a and c above.

3. Some examples of data that are naturally organized as two-dimensional arrays include

    a. the multiplication table.
    b. a table of prime (unfactorable) numbers.
    c. a railroad time table.
    d. a nautical table giving the times of high and low tides at a port city.
    e. only a and c above.

4. Plotting the graph of a function is simpler than displaying a digitized graphic image because
    a. digitized images must first be enhanced before being displayed.
    b. plotting a graph of a function does not use superposition.
    c. with a function there is exactly one y value corresponding to each x value.
    d. the graph of a function does not require the higher resolution and smaller plotted or displayed pixels a digital image does.
    e. none of the above; plotting a function is more complex and time consuming than displaying a digital image.

5. The digital image processing and graph plotting programs are modularized because

    a. the programs would be too long if they were not modularized.
    b. the steps in the processing can be more easily shuffled and recombined if the program is modularized.
    c. the modularization comes about naturally as a result of top-down design of the program.
    d. the program is more easily read and modified when it is modularized.
    e. all but a above.

Part Three: Syntax

Which of the following Fortran statements and declarations are syntactically correct and which are not. Correct the ones that are not correct. Be sure not to change the "intent" of the statements or declarations in the process of correcting them. Assume that correct declarations have been made for all variables, arguments, and parameters used in these statements.

1.
```
REAL ALT (LATMAX, LNGMAX)
```
2.
```
INTEGER MTABLE (1 : 10, 1 : 10)
```
3.
```
CHARACTER CROSWD (1 : 20, 1 : 20) * 1
```
4.
```
LOGICAL (2 : 10, 1 : 15)
```
5.
```
COMPLEX X, Y (1000), Z (1:10, 2:20)
```
6.
```
DOUBLE PRECISION U, V (-10 : 0), W (-20, 20)
```
7.
```
INTEGERS A (5, 12, 13), B (7, 24, 25), SA (3 : 4), SB (5)
```
8.
```
   REAL (A, B, C) (1 : 10, 1 :10)
```
9.
```
DIST ** 2 = (X (1) - X (2)) **2 + (Y (1) - Y (2)) **2 +
+            (Z (1) - Z (2)) **2 - C **2 * (T (1) - T(2)) **2
```
10.
```
TENSOR (I, J) = VECTA (I) * VECTB (J)
```

Part Four: Output

What will be printed when the following programs are run?

1.
```
PROGRAM ONE
CHARACTER IMAGE (1 : 3, 1 : 7, 1 : 10) * 1
CALL BUILD (IMAGE)
CALL NEG (IMAGE)
CALL PRINT (IMAGE)
END
```

```
      SUBROUTINE BUILD (IMAGE)
      CHARACTER IMAGE (1 : 3, 1 : 7, 1 : 10) * 1
      INTEGER DEPTH, LENGTH, WIDTH
      OPEN (UNIT = 1, FILE = 'IMAGIN')
      DO 18 DEPTH = 1, 3
         DO 28 LENGTH = 1, 7
            READ (UNIT = 1, FMT = '(10A1)')
     +                (IMAGE (DEPTH, LENGTH, WIDTH), WIDTH = 1, 10)
  28     CONTINUE
  18 CONTINUE
      END


      SUBROUTINE NEG (IMAGE)
      CHARACTER IMAGE (1 : 3, 1 : 7, 1 : 10) * 1
      INTEGER DEPTH, LENGTH, WIDTH
      DO 18 DEPTH = 1, 3
         DO 28 LENGTH = 1, 7
            DO 38 WIDTH = 1, 10
               IF (IMAGE (DEPTH, LENGTH, WIDTH) .NE. ' ') THEN
                  IMAGE (DEPTH, LENGTH, WIDTH) = ' '
               ELSE
                  IMAGE (DEPTH, LENGTH, WIDTH) = '@'
               END IF
  38        CONTINUE
  28     CONTINUE
  18 CONTINUE
      END


      SUBROUTINE PRINT (IMAGE)
      CHARACTER IMAGE (1 : 3, 1 : 7, 1 : 10) * 1
      INTEGER DEPTH, LENGTH, WIDTH
      DO 18 DEPTH = 1, 3
         DO 28 LENGTH = 1, 7
            PRINT '(10A1)', (IMAGE (DEPTH, LENGTH, WIDTH), WIDTH = 1, 10)
  28     CONTINUE
  18 CONTINUE
      END
```

The input file 'IMAGIN' contains the following lines.

```
[XXXXXXX^X
[-     &&^
[&  ^^($^$
[-    **^*
[X  YYYY^Y
[-  -00-^-
[))-00-*^*
[(X(((((^(
[+     4^4
[& ^*^ &^(
[# #<< <^<
[> >4> >^<
[#     >^(
[XX-XX-X^(
[%%%%%%^%
[$     $^$
[A CDEFG^H
```

```
[I KL  O^P
[- 12+ 4^5
[<    >^6
[XXXXXXX^^
```

2.

```
      PROGRAM TWO
      INTEGER TABLE (1 : 4, 1 : 4)
      CALL BUILD (TABLE)
      CALL DISPLY (TABLE)
      END

      SUBROUTINE BUILD (TABLE)
      INTEGER TABLE (1 : 4, 1 : 4), ROW, COL
      DO 18 ROW = 1, 4
         DO 28 COL = 1, 4
            TABLE (ROW, COL) = ROW ** COL
   28    CONTINUE
   18 CONTINUE
      END

      SUBROUTINE DISPLY (TABLE)
      INTEGER TABLE (1 : 4, 1 : 4), ROW, COL
      DO 18 COL = 1, 4
         PRINT '(4I4)', (TABLE (ROW, COL), ROW = 1, 4)
   18 CONTINUE
      END
```

Part Five: Programming

1. The Problem: A printer image display area 12 rows high by 24 columns
    wide is set aside for displaying a graphic image. Assume that each row is
    approximately twice as high ($1/16$ inch) as each column is wide ($1/12$ inch).
    The graphic to be produced is a circular disk 10 rows high and 20 columns
    wide, centered in the square display area. The Algorithm: The center of
    the display area is at row 6.5 and column 12.5, that is to say midway
    between rows 6 and 7 and columns 12 and 13. The desired circle can be
    obtained by printing an asterisk (*) for each pixels whose distance from row
    6.5 and column 12.5 is less than or equal to 5. The formula for the
    distance between (ROW, COL) and (6.5, 12.5) is

```
      DIST = SQRT ((ROW - 6.5) **2 + 0.25 * (COL - 12.5) **2)
```

Sample Output:

```
RUN CIRCLE

         *******
       *************
     ********************
    *********************
    *********************
    ***********************
    **********************
     *******************
       *************
         *******
```

2. The Problem: In the same 12 × 24 graphics display square as in Problem 1, print a graphic image consisting of 6 successively smaller "concentric" squares converging to the center of the display area. Make each smaller square successively darker. Sample Output:

RUN SQUARS

```
.........................
..———————————————————..
..——++++++++++++++++——..
..——++//////////////++——..
..——++//XXXXXXX//++——..
..——++//XX@@@@XX//++——..
..——++//XX@@@@XX//++——..
..——++//XXXXXXX//++——..
..——++//////////////++——..
..——++++++++++++++++——..
..———————————————————..
.........................
```

Answer Key

Part One: True or False

1. True.

2. True.

3. False, a halftone image has pixels in intermediate shades of gray formed by darkening completely a suitable fraction of the available dots in the pixel.

4. True.

5. False, a constant can be added to each subscript to make the resulting subscript positive. This method was used before the Fortran standard permitted negative subscripts.

Part Two: Multiple Choice

1. a, up to seven-dimensional arrays are permitted by the standard, and some Fortran systems allow more.

2. b is best.

3. e, a table of prime numbers is more naturally stored in a one-dimensional array. d is not a very good answer because there is no natural way to describe what the two subscripts in such a table might be.

4. c, mathematicians love to emphasize that this is the mathematical definition of a function.

5. e; a is false because the program would be a few lines shorter if subroutine calls were not used.

Part Three: Syntax

1.
```
      REAL ALT (LATMAX, LNGMAX)
```
                              <--correct assuming that LATMAX and
                              <--LNGMAX are parameters or dummy
                              <--arguments

2.
```
      INTEGER MTABLE (1 : 10, 1 : 10)
```
                              <--correct

3.
```
      CHARACTER CROSWD (1 : 20, 1 : 20) * 1
```
                              <--correct

4.
```
      LOGICAL VARNAM (2 : 10, 1 : 15)
```
                              <--missing variable name

5.
```
      COMPLEX X, Y (1000), Z (1:10, 2:20)
```
                              <--correct

6.
```
      DOUBLE PRECISION U, V(-10 : 0), W (-20 : 20)
```
                              <--when the default lower bound of 1
                              <--is used, the upper subscript bound
                              <--must be greater than 1 (or equal).

7.

```
     INTEGER A (5, 12, 13), B(7, 24, 25), SA (3 : 4), SB (5)
                              <--the S on the end of INTEGERS would
                              <--be spotted as a duplicate declaration
                              <--for the variable SA
```

8.

```
     REAL A (1 : 10, 1 : 10), B (1 : 10, 1 : 10), C (1 : 10, 1 : 10)
                              <--there is no distributive law of
                              <--declarations
```

9.

```
     DIST = SQRT ((X (1) - X (2)) **2 + (Y (1) - Y (2)) **2 +
     +           (Z (1) = Z (2)) **2 - C **2 * (T (1) - T (2)) **2)
                              <--you can't have an expression on the
                              <--left of the assignment operator
```

10.

```
     TENSOR (I, J) = VECTA (I) * VECTB (J)
                              <--correct, dyadic product of vectors
```

Part Four: Output

1.

RUN ONE

```
aaaaa
aa
aaaa
aa
aa


aaaaa
a   a
a   a
a   a
aaaaa


aaaaa
a
a  aa
a   a
aaaaa
```

2.

RUN TWO

```
    1   2   3   4
    1   4   9  16
    1   8  27  64
    1  16  81 256
```

Part Five: Programming

1.

```
      PROGRAM CIRCLE
C     PLOTS A CIRCLE IN THE MIDDLE OF THE DISPLAY AREA
      CHARACTER IMAGE (1 : 12, 1 : 24) * 1
      CALL BLNKIM (IMAGE)
      CALL DRAW (IMAGE)
      CALL DISPLY (IMAGE)
      END

      SUBROUTINE BLNKIM (IMAGE)
C     BLANKS THE ENTIRE IMAGE AREA
      CHARACTER IMAGE (1 : 12, 1 : 24) * 1
      INTEGER ROW, COL
      DO 18 ROW = 1, 12
         DO 28 COL = 1, 24
            IMAGE (ROW, COL) = ' '
   28    CONTINUE
   18 CONTINUE
      END

      SUBROUTINE DRAW (IMAGE)
C     DARKENS ALL PIXELS WITHIN 5 UNITS OF THE CENTER OF THE DISPLAY AREA
      CHARACTER IMAGE (1 : 12, 1 : 24) * 1
      INTEGER ROW, COL
      REAL DIST
      DO 18 ROW = 1, 12
         DO 28 COL = 1, 24
            DIST = SQRT ((ROW - 6.5) **2 + 0.25 * (COL - 12.5) **2)
            IF (DIST .LE. 5) THEN
               IMAGE (ROW, COL) = '*'
            END IF
   28    CONTINUE
   18 CONTINUE
      END

      SUBROUTINE DISPLY (IMAGE)
C     DISPLAYS THE GRAPHIC IMAGE
      CHARACTER IMAGE (1 : 12, 1 : 24) * 1
      INTEGER ROW, COL
      DO 18 ROW = 1, 12
         PRINT '(24A1)', (IMAGE (ROW, COL), COL = 1, 24)
   18 CONTINUE
      END
```

```
RUN CIRCLE

        *******
     **************
    *****************
   *******************
  *********************
  *********************
  *********************
   *******************
    *****************
     **************
        *******
```

2. This solution uses two of the same subroutines as the previous solution.

```
      PROGRAM SQUARS
C     PRINTS SIX CONCENTRIC SQUARES
      CHARACTER IMAGE (1 : 12, 1 : 24) * 1
      INTEGER CH
      CHARACTER DISPCH (1 : 6) * 1
      DATA (DISPCH (CH), CH = 1, 6) / '.', '-', '+', '/', 'X', '@' /
      CALL BLNKIM (IMAGE)
      DO 18 CH = 1, 6
         CALL SQUARE (IMAGE, CH, DISPCH(CH))
   18 CONTINUE
      CALL DISPLY (IMAGE)
      END

      SUBROUTINE BLNKIM (IMAGE)
C     BLANKS THE ENTIRE IMAGE AREA
      CHARACTER IMAGE (1 : 12, 1 : 24) * 1
      INTEGER ROW, COL
      DO 18 ROW = 1, 12
         DO 28 COL = 1, 24
            IMAGE (ROW, COL) = ' '
   28    CONTINUE
   18 CONTINUE
      END

      SUBROUTINE SQUARE (IMAGE, CH, DISPCH)
C     SUPERPOSES A SQUARE ON THE EXISTING IMAGE
      CHARACTER IMAGE (1 : 12, 1 : 24) * 1, DISPCH * 1
      INTEGER ROW, COL, CH
      DO 18 ROW = CH, 13 - CH
         DO 28 COL = 2 * CH - 1, 26 - 2 * CH
            IMAGE (ROW, COL) = DISPCH
   28    CONTINUE
   18 CONTINUE
      END

      SUBROUTINE DISPLY (IMAGE)
C     DISPLAYS THE GRAPHIC IMAGE
      CHARACTER IMAGE (1 : 12, 1 : 24) * 1
      INTEGER ROW, COL
      DO 18 ROW = 1, 12
         PRINT '(24A1)', (IMAGE (ROW, COL), COL = 1, 24)
```

```
   18 CONTINUE
      END

RUN SQUARS

........................
.._____..
..--++++++++++++++++--..
..--++////////////++--..
..--++//XXXXXXXX//++--..
..--++//XX@@@@XX//++--..
..--++//XX@@@@XX//++--..
..--++//XXXXXXXX//++--..
..--++////////////++--..
..--++++++++++++++++--..
.._____..
........................
```

ADDITIONAL CASE STUDIES 10

Chapter 10 is a collection of interesting applications that do not have to be saved for the end of the semester. They can be presented almost any time after loops have been covered. No new syntactic features of Fortran are introduced in this chapter, so that the focus is entirely on the application.

The sections are independent, except for the use of random number generators from Section 10.3 in Section 10.4. You can do a little or a lot from this chapter or use it for additional examples of programming techniques taught earlier in the semester.

Roundoff

Section 10.1 is a more detailed introduction to roundoff and numerical analysis. If your Fortran system often shows those annoying chains of 9s, for example, $4.99999E-01$ when the answer should have been 0.500000, then you will have to broach the topic early in the semester. If not, you might just want to assign this section as outside reading to the better students.

We are treading here on the fringes of serious numerical problems that prevent perfectly straightforward algorithms from getting the right answers. The difficulty is not so much that there is a roundoff problem, but that the resemblance of user-friendly higher level computer programming languages to English and ordinary mathematics tends to make the programmer believe that computer arithmetic *is* ordinary mathematics.

The examples in this section show this not to be the case. They show simple examples of numeric calculations that don't come out exactly as expected, and in addition, they show programming examples where these small differences between calculated and expected answers can make large differences in the execution of a program. The Self-Test Questions and Programming Exercises keyed to this section provide additional examples.

Deterministic Simulations

Lake Sludge is one of our favorite examples. Because the simulation is deterministic, very little Fortran is required to write the programs. You can use Lake Sludge as an example as early as Chapter 4.

The nice thing about this example is that it may be scaled down, but it is representative of how computers are used to solve real problems. Similar simulations are regularly done for real lakes.

Computer-Assisted Instruction

With all the microcomputers being put in the elementary schools throughout the country, it is nice to know the details of one of the ways they can be used. It is easy to program a computer to conduct routine drill sessions, and that is what Section 10.3 shows.

The major question you and your students should ask yourselves when studying this section is how much better can a computer-assisted instruction program be than the ones we show. The pity is that so many commercially available computer-assisted instruction programs are only marginally better than the ones in this section.

Random and Pseudorandom Numbers

It is amazing that such a simple algorithm as the multiplier-congruence method can generate such good sequences of pseudorandom numbers. The problem we faced, but didn't quite solve to our complete satisfaction was which modulus, multiplier, and adder to present as the official example.

If the modulus is too big, there is overflow on computers with very low ceilings for the size of an integer value. When this happens, the program may either stop (terrible), compute incorrect and unevenly distributed numbers (not good enough for simulations, but probably adequate for computer-assisted instruction), or compute uniformly distributed pseudorandom numbers by dropping the high order bits or digits (wonderful). We opted for a modulus so small that overflow is impossible, even if the maximum integer is 32,767, the smallest we have seen.

There are many fixes that enable a computer with a small maximum integer to calculate a relatively long sequence of pseudorandom numbers in spite of the overflow problem. Many of them tend to be machine specific. There are known methods for multiplying larger numbers to be reduced modulo m without causing overflow, but it didn't seem worth the extra effort to introduce them here. Other methods of skirting the problem, such as using type real arithmetic, also make the function program RNDINT more complicated.

If your computer can handle larger integers, we suggest other, better values for the three parameters in Section 10.4 where better pseudorandom generators are needed.

Nondeterministic Simulations

It certainly takes less time to simulate a gambling game 1000 times than it does to play it 1000 times, and it is usually a lot cheaper. Nondeterministic (also called Monte Carlo) simulations are used to calculate scattering cross sections in particle interactions, nuclear chain reaction parameters, and in other situations where the equations governing the phenomena are too complicated to solve by deterministic techniques. For this reason, some physicists have become experts at generating long, uncorrelated sequences of pseudorandom numbers.

Vocabulary

binary number system
binary computer
computer-assisted instruction
deterministic simulation
equality test with reals
garbage in, garbage out
interactive dialog
mathematical model
Monte Carlo simulation
nondeterministic simulation
nonrepresentable number
probabilistic simulation
pseudorandom number
random number
random integers, generating them
representable number
roundoff error
simulation
truncation

Chapter Outline

No Examination Questions on Chapter 10

Since Chapter 10 contains no new syntactic features and we expect the material to be integrated with other chapters, we have not provided any examination questions. Some of the exercises in the text may provide examination questions, if they are needed.

LIST OF TRANSPARENCY MASTERS

Chapter 1

Chapter 2

Chapter 3

Chapter 6

Chapter 7

T.10.6   416   PROGRAM ROUFIX
                           RUN ROUFIX

A computer is a device with the following capabilities. Some computers have additional capabilities, but all computers have the ones listed below. A computer can

1. Operate automatically without step-by-step human control
2. Perform arithmetic calculations
3. Accept input data
4. Send output data to the user
5. Save data in its memory and later retrieve the data
6. Move data from place to place in its memory
7. Be programmed to execute any meaningful sequence of its built-in operations
8. Choose between programmed alternatives while operating automatically
9. Access its memory in a flexible manner
10. Store its program in the same memory cells that can at other times store data

Table 1.1 A hand calculation that uses memory.

STEP	USER ACTION	DISPLAYED NUMBER
1	Enter 4.567890	4.56789
2	Add	
3	Enter 5.678901	5.678901
4	Equals	10.246791
5	Store displayed number	
6	Enter 2.345678	2.345678
7	Add	
8	Enter 3.456789	3.456789
9	Equals	5.802467
10	Divided by	
11	Recall stored number	10.246791
12	Equals	0.566271625259

Table 1.2 Raising 1.06 to the fifth power on a hand calculator.

STEP	USER ACTION	DISPLAYED NUMBER
1	Enter 1.06	1.06
2	Store displayed number	
3	Multiply by	
4	Recall store number	1.06
5	Equals	1.1236
6	Multiply by	
7	Recall stored number	1.06
8	Equals	1.191016
9	Multiply by	
10	Recall stored number	1.06
11	Equals	1.26247696
12	Multiply by	
13	Recall stored number	1.06
14	Equals	1.3382255776

Table 1.3 A program for raising any number to the fifth power.

PROGRAM STEP	BASIC OPERATION
1	Halt for input (user must enter a number and resume program execution to complete this step)
2	Store displayed number
3	Multiply by
4	Recall stored number
5	Equals
6	Multiply by
7	Recall stored number
8	Equals
9	Multiply by
10	Recall stored number
11	Equals
12	Multiply by
13	Recall stored number
14	Equals
15	Halt so user can read the result

Table 1.4 Using a program twice on a programmable hand calculator.

STEP	USER ACTION	DISPLAYED NUMBER
1	Start program	1.06
2	Enter 1.06 and resume execution	1.06
		1.1236
		1.06
		1.191016
		1.06
		1.26247696
		1.06
		1.3382255776
3	Start program	1.0625
4	Enter 1.0625 and resume execution	1.0625
		1.12890625
		1.0625
		1.199462891
		1.0625
		1.274429321
		1.0625
		1.354081154

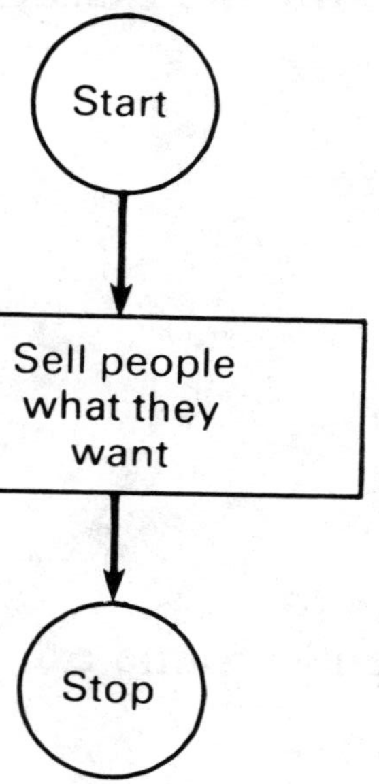

Figure 1.9 How to make a million: the initial inspiration.

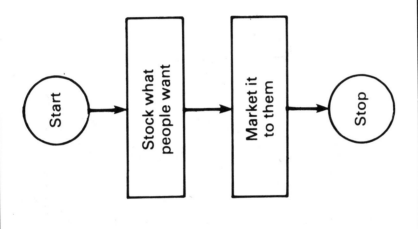

Figure 1.10 This refinement of the initial inspiration to sell something assumes that you will sell a product.

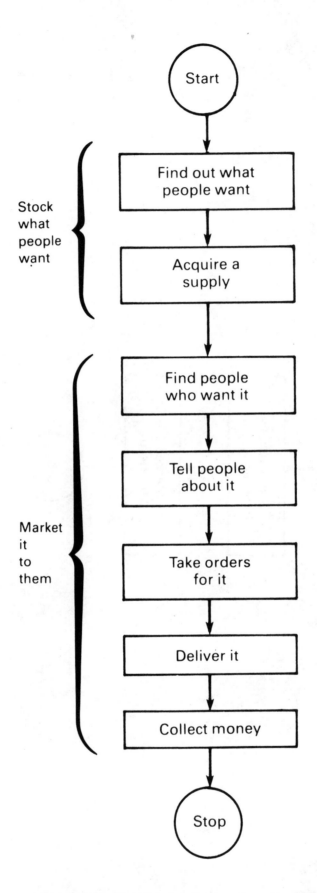

Figure 1.11   A deeper level of refinement.

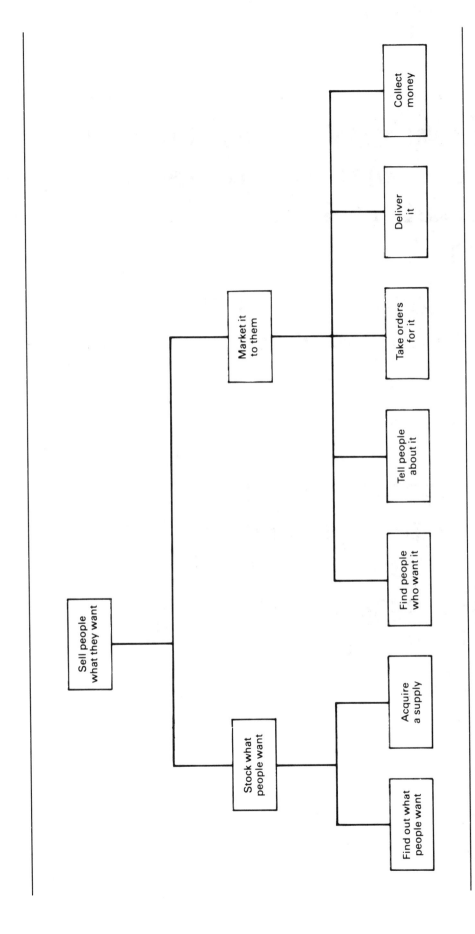

Figure 1.12 Hierarchical organization of subproblems in the task of becoming a millionaire.

```
Program:  Make a Million
   Stock What People Want
   Market It To Them
   end

Subprogram:  Stock What People Want
   Find out what people want
   Acquire a supply
   end


Subprogram:  Market It To Them
   Find people who want it
   Tell people about it
   Take orders for it
   Deliver it
   Collect money
   end
```

RUN PAYROL

        INPUT DATA   NAME: WALT BRAINERD
                      RATE: 9.83000
                      HOURS: 55.0000
                      GROSS PAY = $614.38

        INPUT DATA   NAME: CHARLIE GOLDBERG
                      RATE: 6.29000
                      HOURS: 38.0000
                      GROSS PAY = $239.02

        INPUT DATA   NAME: JONATHAN GROSS
                      RATE: 5.89000
                      HOURS: 17.2500
                      GROSS PAY = $101.60

```
Compute the pay for each employee


For each employee
    Compute the employee's pay


For each employee
    Compute the employee's pay
    Print the pay for the employee


If the employee worked overtime then
    Compute pay by the overtime formula
else
    Compute pay by the regular formula


For each employee
    Obtain employee's name, hourly wage, and hours worked
    Echo the name, hourly wage, and hours worked
    Compute the employee's pay
    Print the pay for the employee


For each employee
    Obtain employee's name, hourly wage, and hours worked
    Echo the name, hourly wage, and hours worked
    If the employee worked overtime then
        Compute pay by the overtime formula
    else
        Compute pay by the regular formula
    Print the pay for the employee
```

```
PROGRAM PAYROL
COMPUTES THE PAYROLL FOR A COMPANY WITH 3 EMPLOYEES.
OVERTIME IS PAID AT TIME-AND-A-HALF.

VARIABLES AND PARAMETERS
    NREMPS = NUMBER OF EMPLOYEES
    EMPLOY = LOOP COUNTER FOR EACH EMPLOYEE
    RATE   = HOURLY PAY RATE
    HOURS  = HOURS WORKED THIS WEEK
    PAY    = GROSS PAY FOR THE WEEK
    REGPAY = PAY FOR THE FIRST 40 HOURS
    OTPAY  = PAY FOR OVERTIME HOURS
    REGHRS = 40 = HOURS IN NORMAL WORK WEEK
    OTHRS  = OVERTIME HOURS
    OTFACT = FACTOR FOR OVERTIME
    NAME   = EMPLOYEE'S NAME


INTEGER NREMPS, EMPLOY
PARAMETER (NREMPS = 3)
REAL RATE, HOURS, PAY
REAL REGPAY, OTHRS, OTPAY
REAL REGHRS, OTFACT
PARAMETER (REGHRS = 40, OTFACT = 1.5)
CHARACTER NAME *20
```

```
FOR EACH EMPLOYEE
DO 18 EMPLOY = 1, NREMPS
   PRINT *
   READ *, NAME, RATE, HOURS
   PRINT *, 'INPUT DATA  NAME:', NAME
   PRINT *, '            RATE:', RATE
   PRINT *, '           HOURS:', HOURS

   COMPUTE THE EMPLOYEE'S PAY
   IF (HOURS .GT. REGHRS) THEN
      COMPUTE PAY BY THE OVERTIME FORMULA
      REGPAY = RATE * REGHRS
      OTHRS = HOURS - REGHRS
      OTPAY = OTFACT * RATE * OTHRS
      PAY = REGPAY + OTPAY
   ELSE
      COMPUTE PAY BY THE OVERTIME FORMULA
      PAY = RATE * HOURS
   ENDIF
   PRINT '(T15, A, F6.2)',
  +         'GROSS PAY = $', PAY
18 CONTINUE
   END
```

General form of a Fortran program:

PROGRAM *program name*
Fortran statements
. . .
END

Example:

```
PROGRAM CALC1
PRINT *, 84 + 13
END
```

PRINT statement

General Form:

PRINT *format* , *list of expressions to be printed*

Example:

```
PRINT *, 'THE ANSWER IS ', (92 + 12) / 2
```

```
        PROGRAM QUOTES
        PRINT *, '84 + 13'
        END

RUN QUOTES


  84 + 13



        PROGRAM HELLO
        PRINT *, 'HELLO, I AM A COMPUTER.'
        END

RUN HELLO


  HELLO, I AM A COMPUTER.



        PROGRAM CLC1V2
        PRINT *, '84 + 13 =', 84 + 13
        END

RUN CLC1V2


  84 + 13 =  97
```

$$4 + 12 / 2 - 1 + 5 * 3 ** 2$$
$$= 4 + 12 / 2 - 1 + 5 * 9$$
$$= 4 + 6 - 1 + 5 * 9$$
$$= 4 + 6 - 1 + 45$$
$$= 10 - 1 + 45$$
$$= 9 + 45$$
$$= 54$$

$$432 / 12 / 6 / 3$$
$$= 36 / 6 / 3$$
$$= 6 / 3$$
$$= 2$$

$$12 / 6 * 2$$
$$= 2 * 2$$
$$= 4$$

```
PROGRAM ADD2
INTEGER X, Y
READ *, X
PRINT *, 'INPUT DATA  X:', X
READ *, Y
PRINT *, 'INPUT DATA  Y:', Y
PRINT *, 'X + Y =', X + Y
END


RUN ADD2

   INPUT DATA  X:  84
   INPUT DATA  Y:  13
   X + Y =  97
```

```
PROGRAM AVG4V3
REAL A, B, C, D
READ *, A, B, C, D
PRINT *, 'INPUT DATA  A:', A
PRINT *, '             B:', B
PRINT *, '             C:', C
PRINT *, '             D:', D
PRINT *, 'AVERAGE =', (A + B + C + D) / 4
END
```

58.5
60
61.3
57

RUN AVG4V3

```
   INPUT DATA  A:    58.5000
               B:    60.0000
               C:    61.3000
               D:    57.0000
   AVERAGE =    59.2000
```

Table 2.1 Acceptable Variable Names in Fortran.

LISA, PAMELA, JULIE	usual names
ANSWER, NUMBER, VALUE	English words
ANFANG, ESPRIT, MUCHO	foreign words
X3J9, W3KT, YHV93X, EXPO67	mixed alphabetic and numeric

Table 2.2 Unacceptable Variable Names in Fortran.

6AU8, 14U2	starting with a digit
E/L/O, MANY%, A−1	characters other than letters or digits
SERENDIPITY, SITZMARK	more than six characters

```
      PROGRAM SNDWCH
C     COMPUTES THE COST OF A PEANUT BUTTER
C     AND JELLY SANDWICH USING TWO SLICES OF BREAD,
C     .0625 JARS OF PEANUT BUTTER, AND .03125 JARS OF JELLY

      REAL LOFBRD, PBUTTR, JELLY, SLCBRD, CSTSND, SLICES


      PARAMETER (
     +    LOFBRD = .59,
     +    PBUTTR = 1.65,
     +    JELLY = 1.29,
     +    SLICES = 16.0 )

      SLCBRD = LOFBRD / SLICES
      CSTSND = 2 * SLCBRD + .0625 * PBUTTR + .03125 * JELLY
      PRINT *, 'A PEANUT BUTTER AND JELLY SANDWICH COSTS $',
     +    CSTSND
      PRINT *, 'PRICES ARE SUBJECT TO CHANGE AT ANY TIME'
      PRINT *, '  WITHOUT WRITTEN NOTICE.'
      END
RUN SNDWCH

  A PEANUT BUTTER AND JELLY SANDWICH COSTS $  0.217187
  PRICES ARE SUBJECT TO CHANGE AT ANY TIME
    WITHOUT WRITTEN NOTICE.
```

```
PROGRAM WHO
CHARACTER WHATS *20

    PRINT *, 'DO I REMEMBER WHATSHISNAME?'
    READ *, WHATS
    PRINT *, 'OF COURSE, I REMEMBER', WHATS
    END

RUN WHO

    DO I REMEMBER WHATSHISNAME?
OF COURSE, I REMEMBER ROGER KAPUTNIK

'ROGER KAPUTNIK'
```

```
        PRINT '(F5.1, A, I4)', X, ' AND ', N

        FMT = '(F5.1, A, I4)'
        PRINT FMT, X, ' AND ', N

        PRINT 15, X, ' AND ' N
   15   FORMAT (F5.1, A, I4)
```

6.3 AND -26

```
      PRINT '(3I2)', 2, 3, 4

  2 3 4


      X = 7.346E-9
      PRINT 25, ' THE ANSWER IS ', X
   25  FORMAT (A, E10.3)

THE ANSWER IS    .735E-08


      Q1 = 5.6
      Q2 = 5.73
      Q3 = 5.79
      F123 = '(A, 3(/, T2, A, I1, A, F3.1))'
      PRINT F123, ' HERE COME THE ANSWERS--',
   +        ' Q', 1, '=', Q1,
   +        ' Q', 2, '=', Q2,
   +        ' Q', 3, '=', Q3

HERE COME THE ANSWERS--
Q1=5.6
Q2=5.7
Q3=5.8
```

```
       REAL X1, X2, X3
       INTEGER J1, J2, J3
       CHARACTER C *4
       READ 35, C, X1, J1, X2, J2, X3, J3
  35   FORMAT (A, 3 (F2.1, I1))
```

1234567890123

C = '1234'
X1 = 5.6
J1 = 7
X2 = 8.9
J2 = 0
X3 = 1.2
J3 = 3

Built-in functions:

Built-in functions provide a collection of operations that can be performed on data of all types. The following table lists many of the commonly used built-in functions.

1	INT	convert to integer
2	REAL	convert to real
3	NINT	convert to nearest integer
4	ABS	absolute value
5	MIN	minimum
6	MAX	maximum
7	SQRT	square root
8	MOD	remainder
9	LOG10	logarithm base 10
10	LOG	logarithm base e
11	EXP	exponential
12	SIN	sine
13	COS	cosine
14	TAN	tangent
15	ASIN	arcsine
16	ACOS	arccosine
17	ATAN	arctangent
18	SINH	hyperbolic sine
19	COSH	hyperbolic cosine
20	TANH	hyperbolic tangent

MOD (A1, A2) = A1 - INT (A1 / A2) * A2

For example,

MOD (17, 5) = 2
MOD (-17, 5)
    = -17 - INT (-17 / 5) * 5
    = -17 - (-3) * 5
    = -17 + 15
    = -2
MOD (17, -5)
    = 17 - (-3) * (-5)
    = +17 - 15
    = 2
MOD (6.8, 2.1)
    = 6.8 - INT (6.8 / 2.1) * 2.1
    = 6.8 - 3 * 2.1
    = 6.8 - 6.3
    = 0.5

```
PROGRAM SUB2
INTEGER X, Y
PRINT *, 'INPUT DATA  X:'
READ *, X
PRINT *, 'INPUT DATA  Y:'
READ *, Y
PRINT *, 'X - Y = ', X - Y
END
```

RUN SUB2

```
  INPUT DATA  X:
83
  INPUT DATA  Y:
67
  X - Y =    16
```

```fortran
      PROGRAM QUAD
C     CALCULATES AND PRINTS THE ROOTS OF A QUADRATIC EQUATION

C     VARIABLES:
C        A, B, C: COEFFICIENTS
C        X1, X2: ROOTS

      REAL A, B, C, X1, X2

C     READ THE COEFFICIENTS
      PRINT *, 'ENTER A, THE COEFFICIENT OF X **2'
      READ *, A
      PRINT *, 'ENTER B, THE COEFFICIENT OF X'
      READ *, B
      PRINT *, 'ENTER C, THE CONSTANT TERM'
      READ *, C

C     CALCULATE THE ROOTS BY THE QUADRATIC FORMULA
      X1 = (-B + SQRT (B ** 2 - 4 * A * C)) / (2 * A)
      X2 = (-B - SQRT (B ** 2 - 4 * A * C)) / (2 * A)

C     PRINT THE ROOTS
      PRINT *, 'THE ROOTS ARE'
      PRINT *, 'X1 =', X1
      PRINT *, 'X2 =', X2
      END
```

T 2.15

```
RUN QUAD

  ENTER A, THE COEFFICIENT OF X **2
1

  ENTER B, THE COEFFICIENT OF X
-5
  ENTER C, THE CONSTANT TERM
6
  THE ROOTS ARE
  X1 =   3.00000
  X2 =   2.00000


RUN QUAD

  ENTER A, THE COEFFICIENT OF X **2
4
  ENTER B, THE COEFFICIENT OF X
8
  ENTER C, THE CONSTANT TERM
-21
  THE ROOTS ARE
  X1 =   1.50000
  X2 =  -3.50000


RUN QUAD

  ENTER A, THE COEFFICIENT OF X **2
1
  ENTER B, THE COEFFICIENT OF X
-1
  ENTER C, THE CONSTANT TERM
-1
  THE ROOTS ARE
  X1 =   1.61803
  X2 =  -0.618034
```

RUN QUAD

  ENTER A, THE COEFFICIENT OF X **2
1
  ENTER B, THE COEFFICIENT OF X
-6
  ENTER C, THE CONSTANT TERM
9
  THE ROOTS ARE
  X1 =   3.00000
  X2 =   3.00000

RUN QUAD

  ENTER A, THE COEFFICIENT OF X **2
1
  ENTER B, THE COEFFICIENT OF X
0
  ENTER C, THE CONSTANT TERM
1
***** ERROR: ATTEMPT TO TAKE THE SQUARE ROOT OF A NEGATIVE QUANTITY *****
***** EXECUTION TERMINATED *****

```
      PROGRAM PENDLM
C     CALCULATES THE FREQUENCY AND PERIOD
C     OF A PENDULUM OF LENGTH L

      REAL L, F, T, PI, G
      PARAMETER (PI = 3.14159,
                 G = 9.80665)

      READ *, L
      PRINT *, 'INPUT DATA L: ', L
      F = (1.0 / 2.0 * PI) SQRT (G / L)
      T = 1.0 / F
      END
```

```
RUN PENDLM
  *** ERROR -- SYNTAX ERROR IN PARAMETER STATEMENT ***
  PARAMETER (PI = 3.14159,
  *** MISSING PARAMETER ASSIGNMENT ***

  *** ERROR -- SYNTAX ERROR IN ASSIGNMENT STATEMENT ***
  G = 9.80665)
  *** UNMATCHED PARENTHESES ***

  *** ERROR -- SYNTAX ERROR IN ASSIGNMENT STATEMENT ***
  F = (1.0 / 2.0 * PI) SQRT (G / L)
  *** EXPECTING OPERATOR WHEN SQRT FOUND ***

  *** SEVERE ERRORS -- NO EXECUTION ***
```

General form of an **IF Block:**

    IF (*logical expression*) THEN
        statements
    ELSE IF (*logical expression*) THEN
        statements

    ELSE IF (*logical expression*) THEN
        statements
    ELSE IF . . .
            .
            .
            .
    ELSE
        statements
    END IF

The ELSE IF clauses are optional and may be omitted as may be the ELSE clause. The END IF must not be omitted.

Examples:

```
IF (A .GT. B) THEN
    TEMP = A
    A = B
    B = TEMP
ELSE IF (A .LT. B) THEN
    PRINT *, 'B IS BIGGER'
ELSE
    PRINT *, 'THEY ARE THE SAME'
END IF

IF (A .EQ. B) THEN
    C = A
    PRINT *, C
END IF
```

Caution: The comparison operator for equality (.EQ.) is not the same as the assignment operator (=).

Table 3.1 Fortran symbols for the comparison operators.

Mathematical symbol	Fortran symbol	English equivalent
<	.LT.	is less than
>	.GT.	is greater than
=	.EQ.	is equal to
≤	.LE.	is less than or equal to
≥	.GE.	is greater than or equal to
≠	.NE.	is not equal to

```fortran
      PROGRAM ESCAPE
C     ACCEPTS AS INPUT AN INITIAL VELOCITY V
C     PRINTS MAXIMUM HEIGHT ATTAINED,
C       IF OBJECT DOES NOT ESCAPE EARTH
C     PRINTS FINAL ESCAPE VELOCITY, VFINAL,
C       IF OBJECT ESCAPES

C     PARAMETERS
C       G = ACCELERATION OF GRAVITY NEAR EARTH'S SURFACE
C             (IN METERS / SEC ** 2)
C       RE = RADIUS OF THE EARTH (IN METERS)

      REAL V, H, VFINAL, G, RE
      PARAMETER (G = 9.80, RE = 6.366E6)

      READ *, V
      PRINT *, 'INITIAL VELOCITY OF OBJECT =', V, 'METERS / SEC'
      IF (V ** 2 .LT. 2 * G * RE) THEN
         H = RE / (1 - V ** 2 / (2 * G * RE))
         PRINT *, 'THE OBJECT ATTAINS A MAXIMUM HEIGHT OF', H - RE, 'METERS'
         PRINT *, 'ABOVE THE EARTH''S SURFACE BEFORE RETURNING TO EARTH.'
      ELSE IF (V ** 2 .EQ. 2 * G * RE) THEN
         PRINT *, 'THIS VELOCITY IS THE ESCAPE VELOCITY OF THE EARTH.'
         PRINT *, 'THE OBJECT JUST BARELY ESCAPES FROM EARTH''S GRAVITY.'
      ELSE
         VFINAL = SQRT (V ** 2 - 2 * G * RE)
         PRINT *, 'THE OBJECT ESCAPES FROM EARTH WITH A VELOCITY OF',
     +            VFINAL, 'METERS / SEC.'
      END IF
      END
```

RUN ESCAPE

INITIAL VELOCITY OF OBJECT =   1000.00 METERS / SEC
THE OBJECT ATTAINS A MAXIMUM HEIGHT OF   51432.5 METERS
ABOVE THE EARTH'S SURFACE BEFORE RETURNING TO EARTH.

RUN ESCAPE

INITIAL VELOCITY OF OBJECT =   20000.0 METERS / SEC
THE OBJECT ESCAPES FROM EARTH WITH A VELOCITY OF   16589.9 METERS / SEC.

RUN ESCAPE

INITIAL VELOCITY OF OBJECT =   11170.0 METERS / SEC
THE OBJECT ATTAINS A MAXIMUM HEIGHT OF   1.69255E+11 METERS
ABOVE THE EARTH'S SURFACE BEFORE RETURNING TO EARTH.

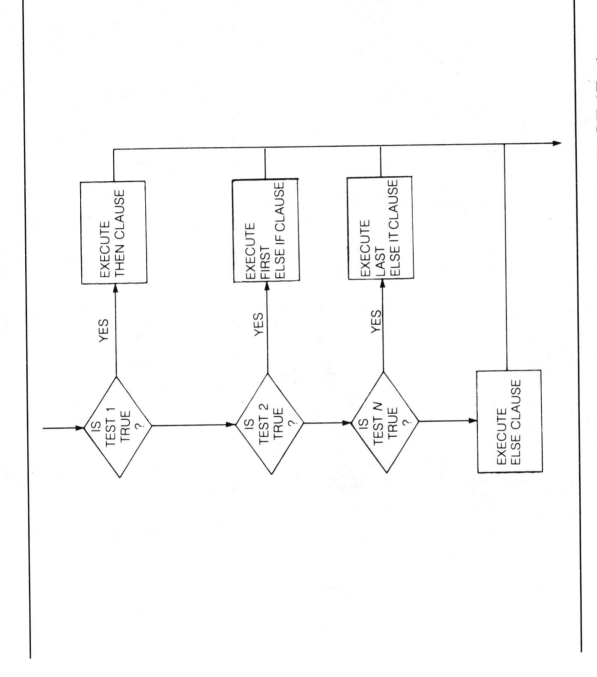

Figure 3.1 Flowchart for an IF block containing ELSE IF clauses.

```
IF (hours worked > 40) THEN
    Calculate pay by the overtime formula
ELSE
    Calculate pay by the regular formula
END IF
```

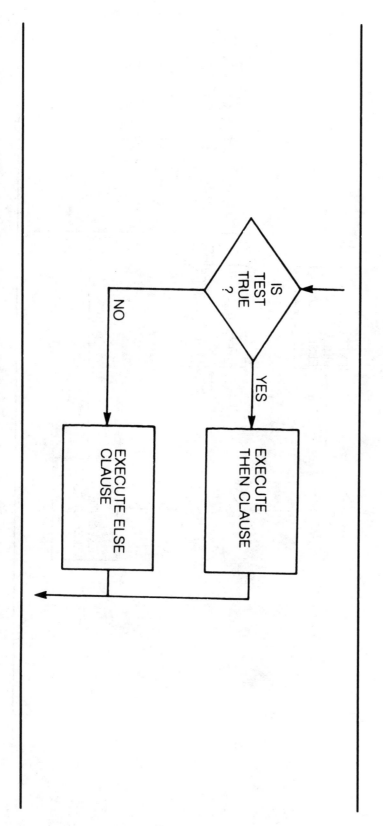

Figure 3.2 Flowchart for an IF block with two alternatives.

```
      PROGRAM XPOS
      INTEGER X
      READ *, X
      PRINT *, 'INPUT DATA  X:', X

      IF (X .LT. 0) THEN
         X = -X
      END IF
      PRINT *, 'ABSOLUTE VALUE =', X
      END
RUN XPOS

  INPUT DATA  X:  -5
  ABSOLUTE VALUE =  5


RUN XPOS

  INPUT DATA  X:  7
  ABSOLUTE VALUE =  7
```

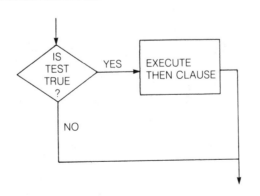

Figure 3.3 Flowchart for an IF block with no ELSE IF or ELSE clauses.

```
C        FIND APPROPRIATE RANGE AND COMPUTE TAX
         IF (INCOME .EQ. 0) THEN
            TAX = 0
            BRAKET = 0
         ELSE IF (INCOME .GT. 0 .AND. INCOME .LE. 500) THEN
            TAX = 0.14 * INCOME
            BRAKET = 14
         ELSE IF (INCOME .GT. 500 .AND. INCOME .LE. 1000) THEN
            TAX = 70 + 0.15 * (INCOME - 500)
            BRAKET = 14
         ELSE IF (INCOME .GT. 1000 .AND. INCOME .LE. 1500) THEN
            TAX = 145 + 0.16 * (INCOME - 1000)
            BRAKET = 16
         ELSE IF (INCOME .GT. 1500 .AND. INCOME .LE. 2000) THEN
            TAX = 225 + 0.17 * (INCOME - 1500)
            BRAKET = 17
         ELSE IF (INCOME .GT. 2000 .AND. INCOME .LE. 4000) THEN
            TAX = 310 + 0.19 * (INCOME - 2000)
            BRAKET = 19
         ELSE IF (INCOME .GT. 4000 .AND. INCOME .LE. 6000) THEN
            TAX = 690 + 0.21 * (INCOME - 4000)
            BRAKET = 21
         ELSE IF (INCOME .GT. 6000 .AND. INCOME .LE. 8000) THEN
            TAX = 1110 + 0.24 * (INCOME - 6000)
            BRAKET = 24
         ELSE IF (INCOME .GT. 8000 .AND. INCOME .LE. 10000) THEN
            TAX = 1590 + 0.25 * (INCOME - 8000)
            BRAKET = 25
         END IF
C        END OF TAX COMPUTATION SECTION
```

```fortran
      LOGICAL YES, NO, DONE, FOUND, MISSING, QUIT
      INTEGER NEWX, OLDX, COUNT

      PARAMETER (YES = .TRUE., NO = .FALSE.)
      DONE = .TRUE.
      FOUND = (NEWX .EQ. OLDX)
      MISSING = .NOT. FOUND

      QUIT = (NEWX .GT. OLDX) .AND. .NOT. FOUND

      IF ((NEWX .EQ. OLDX) .OR. (COUNT .GT. 100)) THEN
         PRINT *, 'QUITING'
      ELSE
         PRINT *, 'CONTINUING'
      END IF
```

```
C         FIND APPROPRIATE RANGE AND COMPUTE TAX
          IF (INCOME .EQ. 0) THEN
              TAX = 0
              BRAKET = 0
          ELSE IF (INCOME .LE. 500) THEN
              TAX = 0.14 * INCOME
              BRAKET = 14
          ELSE IF (INCOME .LE. 1000) THEN
              TAX = 70 + 0.15 * (INCOME - 500)
              BRAKET = 14
          ELSE IF (INCOME .LE. 1500) THEN
              TAX = 145 + 0.16 * (INCOME - 1000)
              BRAKET = 16
          ELSE IF (INCOME .LE. 2000) THEN
              TAX = 225 + 0.17 * (INCOME - 1500)
              BRAKET = 17
          ELSE IF (INCOME .LE. 4000) THEN
              TAX = 310 + 0.19 * (INCOME - 2000)
              BRAKET = 19
          ELSE IF (INCOME .LE. 6000) THEN
              TAX = 690 + 0.21 * (INCOME - 4000)
              BRAKET = 21
          ELSE IF (INCOME .LE. 8000) THEN
              TAX = 1110 + 0.24 * (INCOME - 6000)
              BRAKET = 24
          ELSE IF (INCOME .LE. 10000) THEN
              TAX = 1590 + 0.25 * (INCOME - 8000)
              BRAKET = 25
          END IF
C         END OF TAX COMPUTATION SECTION
```

```
IF (BONUS1 .EQ. RIGHT) THEN
    IF (BONUS2 .EQ. RIGHT) THEN
        IF (BONUS3 .EQ. RIGHT) THEN
            SCORE = SCORE + 5
        END IF
    END IF
END IF
```

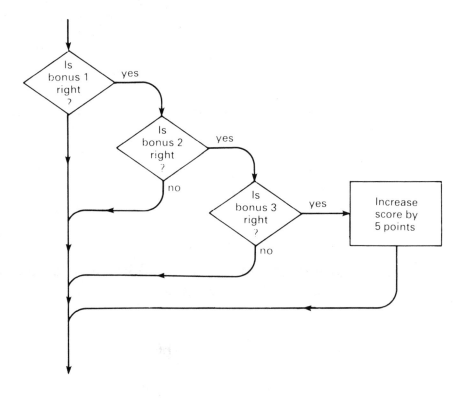

Figure 3.4 Nested IF block structure of the program XTRA2B. All three IF conditions must be satisfied to earn the 5-point bonus.

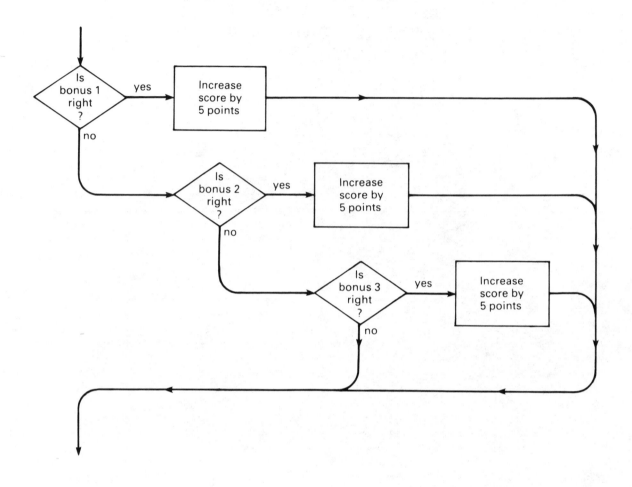

Figure 3.5 IF block structure of the program XTRA3B. The 5-point bonus is awarded if any of the three bonus questions is answered correctly.

```
IF (BONUS1 .EQ. RIGHT) THEN
   SCORE = SCORE + 5
ELSE IF (BONUS2 .EQ. RIGHT) THEN
   SCORE = SCORE + 5
ELSE IF (BONUS3 .EQ. RIGHT) THEN
   SCORE = SCORE + 5
END IF

PRINT *, 'ADJUSTED EXAM SCORE =', SCORE
END
```

```
      PROGRAM QUAD2

C     CALCULATES AND PRINTS THE ROOTS OF A QUADRATIC FORMULA
C     EVEN IF THEY ARE COMPLEX

C     VARIABLES:  A, B, C = COEFFICIENTS
C                 X1, X2 = REAL ROOTS
C                 D = DISCRIMINANT
C                 REALX, IMAGX = REAL AND IMAGINARY PARTS
C                                     OF COMPLEX ROOTS

      REAL A, B, C, X1, X2, D, REALX, IMAGX
C     READ THE COEFFICIENTS
      READ *, A, B, C
      PRINT *, 'ECHO OF INPUT DATA  A:', A
      PRINT *, '                    B:', B
      PRINT *, '                    C:', C

C     CALCULATE THE ROOTS
      D = B **2 - 4 * A * C
      IF (D .GE. 0) THEN
C         USE REAL FORM OF QUADRATIC FORMULA FOR THE ROOTS
          X1 = (-B + SQRT (D)) / ( 2 * A)
          X2 = (-B - SQRT (D)) / ( 2 * A)
          PRINT *, 'THE ROOTS ARE REAL'
          PRINT *, 'X1 =', X1
          PRINT *, 'X2 =', X2
      ELSE
C         USE COMPLEX FORM OF QUADRATIC FORMULA FOR ROOTS
          REALX = -B / (2 * A)
          IMAGX = SQRT (ABS (D)) / (2 * A)
          PRINT *, 'THE ROOTS ARE COMPLEX'
          PRINT *, 'X1 = ', REALX, '+', IMAGX, 'I'
          PRINT *, 'X2 = ', REALX, '-', IMAGX, 'I'
      END IF
      END
```

```
      PROGRAM QUAD3

C     CALCULATES AND PRINTS THE ROOTS OF A QUADRATIC FORMULA
C     EVEN IF THEY ARE COMPLEX

C     VARIABLES:  A, B, C = COEFFICIENTS
C                 CA, CB, CC = COMPLEX COEFFICIENTS
C                 Z1, Z2 = ROOTS

      REAL A, B, C
      COMPLEX CA, CB, CC, Z1, Z2

C     READ THE COEFFICIENTS
      READ *, A, B, C
      PRINT *, 'ECHO OF INPUT DATA  A:', A
      PRINT *, '                    B:', B
      PRINT *, '                    C:', C

C     CONVERT COEFFICIENTS TO TYPE COMPLEX
      CA = CMPLX (A)
      CB = CMPLX (B)
      CC = CMPLX (C)

C     CALCULATE THE ROOTS
      Z1 = (-CB + SQRT (CB ** 2 - 4 * CA * CC)) / (2 * CA)
      Z2 = (-CB - SQRT (CB ** 2 - 4 * CA * CC)) / (2 * CA)

C     PRINT THE ROOTS
      PRINT *, 'THE ROOTS ARE:'
      PRINT *, 'Z1 =', Z1
      PRINT *, 'Z2 =', Z2
      END
```

RUN QUAD3

    ECHO OF INPUT DATA   A: 1.00000
                         B: 0.
                         C: 1.00000
    THE ROOTS ARE:
    Z1 = (0.,   1.00000)
    Z2 = (0.,   -1.00000)
RUN QUAD3

    ECHO OF INPUT DATA   A: 4.00000
                         B: 8.00000
                         C: -21.0000
    THE ROOTS ARE:
    Z1 = (1.50000, 0.)
    Z2 = (-3.50000, 0.)

Table 3.3 The collating sequence for a selection of printable ASCII characters.

blank ! " # $ % & ' ( ) * + , - . /
0 1 2 3 4 5 6 7 8 9 : ; < = > ? @
A B C D E F G H I J K L M N O P Q R S T U V W X Y Z [ ] ^ _ `
a b c d e f g h i j k l m n o p q r s t u v w x y z { | } ~

Table 3.4 The collating sequence for a selection of printable EBCDIC characters.

blank] . < (+ ! & [$ *) ; ^ - / , % _ > ? : # @ ' = "
a b c d e f g h i j k l m n o p q r s t u v w x y z
A B C D E F G H I J K L M N O P Q R S T U V W X Y Z
0 1 2 3 4 5 6 7 8 9

Table 3.5 A Computer Printout of the ASCII Character Set.

	0	1	2	3	4	5	6	7
	0	1	2	3	4	5	6	7
	8	9	10	11	12	13	14	15
	16	17	18	19	20	21	22	23
	24	25	26	27	28	29	30	31
	32	33 !	34 "	35 #	36 $	37 %	38 &	39 '
	40 (	41)	42 *	43 +	44 ,	45 -	46 .	47 /
	48 0	49 1	50 2	51 3	52 4	53 5	54 6	55 7
	56 8	57 9	58 :	59 ;	60 <	61 =	62 >	63 ?
	64 @	65 A	66 B	67 C	68 D	69 E	70 F	71 G
	72 H	73 I	74 J	75 K	76 L	77 M	78 N	79 O
	80 P	81 Q	82 R	83 S	84 T	85 U	86 V	87 W
	88 X	89 Y	90 Z	91 [	92	93]	94 ^	95 _
	96 `	97 a	98 b	99 c	100 d	101 e	102 f	103 g
	104 h	105 i	106 j	107 k	108 l	109 m	110 n	111 o
	112 p	113 q	114 r	115 s	116 t	117 u	118 v	119 w
	120 x	121 y	122 z	123 {	124		125 }	126 ~	127 ●

T 3.17

```fortran
      PROGRAM BUYDSK
C     CALCULATES THE COST OF FLOPPY DISKS ORDERED BY MAIL

      INTEGER DISKS, BOXES
      REAL PRICE, PRCBOX, SHIPNG
      PARAMETER (SHIPNG = 1.50)


      READ *, DISKS
      PRINT *, 'INPUT DATA  DISKS:', DISKS
      IF (MOD (DISKS, 10) .NE. 0) THEN
         PRINT *, 'NOT AN EXACT NUMBER OF BOXES'
         PRINT *, 'ORDER CANCELLED'
      ELSE
         BOXES = DISKS / 10

C        DETERMINE PRICE PER BOX
         IF (BOXES .GE. 10) THEN
            PRCBOX = 16.60
         ELSE IF (BOXES .LT. 10) THEN
            PRCBOX = 19.30
         ELSE IF (BOXES .LT. 5) THEN
            PRCBOX = 21.50
         END IF

C        CALCULATE PRICE OF DISKS (INCLUDING SHIPPING AND HANDLING)
         PRICE = BOXES * PRCBOX + SHIPNG

         PRINT '(A, F6.2)', '  THE DISKS COST $', PRICE
         PRINT *, 'INCLUDING SHIPPING AND HANDLING'
      END IF
      END
```

T 3.18

DO Block:

General Form:

DO *label variable* = *expression, expression, expression*

       statement

       . . .

       statement

  label CONTINUE

Examples:

```
    DO 18 N = 1, 20
       PRINT *, N
18  CONTINUE
    DO 28 VALUE = 20.0, 0.1, -0.1
       SUM = SUM + VALUE
28  CONTINUE
```

Step Size:

In Fortran, successive values of a DO variable may increase or decrease by any amount. The step size is one if none is given in the DO statement.

```
C       PROGRAM SQUARS
        PRINTS A TABLE OF SQUARES AND SQUARE ROOTS

        INTEGER NUMBER

        PRINT 15, 'NUMBER', 'SQUARE', 'SQUARE ROOT'
15      FORMAT (2A10, A15)

        DO 28 NUMBER = 1, 10
        PRINT 25, NUMBER, NUMBER ** 2, SQRT (REAL (NUMBER))
25      FORMAT (2I10, F15.3)
28      CONTINUE
        END

RUN SQUARS

    NUMBER      SQUARE      SQUARE ROOT
         1           1            1.000
         2           4            1.414
         3           9            1.732
         4          16            2.000
         5          25            2.236
         6          36            2.449
         7          49            2.646
         8          64            2.828
         9          81            3.000
        10         100            3.162
```

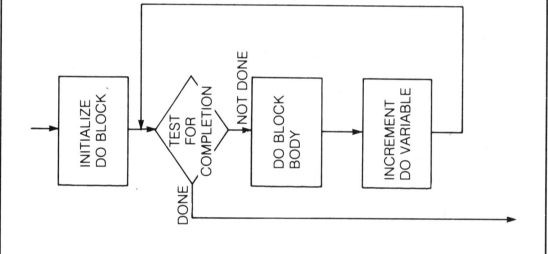

Figure 4.2 Flowchart for a DO Block.

```
      PROGRAM MULT5
C     PRINTS ALL MULTIPLES OF 5
C     THAT ARE <= 45 AND NOT MULTIPLES OF 3

      INTEGER N

      DO 18 N = 5, 45, 5
         IF (MOD (N, 3) .NE. 0) THEN
            PRINT *, N
         END IF
   18 CONTINUE
      END


      RUN MULT5

         5
         10
         20
         25
         35
         40
```

DO Block with Exit:

General Form:

```
        DO label variable = expression, expression, expression
            statements
            IF (exit condition) THEN
                GO TO label2
            END IF
            statements
label   CONTINUE
label2  ...
```

Example:

```
        DO 18 N = 1, 1000
            READ *, NUMBER
            IF (NUMBER .EQ. SIGNAL) THEN
                GO TO 19
            PRINT *, NUMBER
            END IF
18      CONTINUE
19      ...
```

```
      PROGRAM DOWHIL
C     COUNT THE NUMBER OF SCORES USING A DO WHILE BLOCK CONSTRUCT
C     DO NOT COUNT THE SIGNAL AT THE END OF THE INPUT

      INTEGER LINE, NUMBER, COUNT, SIGNAL
      PARAMETER (SIGNAL = -1)

      COUNT = 0
      READ *, NUMBER
      PRINT *, 'INPUT DATA:  NUMBER', NUMBER

C     DO WHILE (NUMBER .NE. SIGNAL)
      DO 18 LINE = 1, 10000
         IF (NUMBER .EQ. SIGNAL) THEN
            GO TO 19
         END IF
         COUNT = COUNT + 1
         READ *, NUMBER
         PRINT *, 'INPUT DATA:  NUMBER', NUMBER
18    CONTINUE
19    PRINT *
      PRINT *, 'THERE ARE', COUNT, 'SCORES.'
      END
```

```
      PROGRAM AVG27B
C     CALCULATE THE AVERAGE TEST SCORE
C     IN A CLASS WITH 27 STUDENTS

      INTEGER NUMSCR, COUNT
      REAL SUM, SCORE
      PARAMETER (NUMSCR = 27)

      SUM = 0
      DO 18 COUNT = 1, NUMSCR
         READ *, SCORE
         PRINT *, 'INPUT DATA  SCORE: ', SCORE
         SUM = SUM + SCORE
   18 CONTINUE

      PRINT *, 'AVERAGE TEST SCORE = ', SUM / NUMSCR
      END
```

Table 4.1 Values of the variables SCORE and SUM during execution of the program AVG27B using data from the sample run.

SCORE	SUM	PASS THROUGH THE DO BLOCK
undefined	0.0	before the 1st pass
85.0	85.0	after the 1st pass
97.0	182.0	after the 2nd pass
68.0	250.0	after the 3rd pass
86.0	336.0	after the 4th pass
75.0	411.0	after the 5th pass
90.0	501.0	after the 6th pass
82.0	583.0	after the 7th pass
100.0	683.0	after the 8th pass
87.0	770.0	after the 9th pass
63.0	833.0	after the 10th pass
79.0	912.0	after the 11th pass
85.0	997.0	after the 12th pass
93.0	1090.0	after the 13th pass
62.0	1152.0	after the 14th pass
88.0	1240.0	after the 15th pass
76.0	1316.0	after the 16th pass
38.0	1354.0	after the 17th pass
70.0	1424.0	after the 18th pass
87.0	1511.0	after the 19th pass
93.0	1604.0	after the 20th pass
98.0	1702.0	after the 21st pass
81.0	1783.0	after the 22nd pass
95.0	1878.0	after the 23rd pass
72.0	1950.0	after the 24th pass
89.0	2039.0	after the 25th pass
99.0	2138.0	after the 26th pass
84.0	2222.0	after the 27th pass

```
      PROGRAM TWOSUM
C     TESTS WHETHER THE ASCENDING SUM 1+2+3+...+N
C     IS EQUAL TO THE DESCENDING SUM N+(N-1)+...+2+1

      INTEGER N, J, SUM

      READ *, N
      PRINT *, 'INPUT DATA  N:', N

      SUM = 0
      DO 18 J = 1, N
         SUM = SUM + J
 18   CONTINUE
      PRINT *, 'THE ASCENDING SUM IS', SUM

      DO 28 J = N, 1
         SUM = SUM + J
 28   CONTINUE
      PRINT *, 'THE DESCENDING SUM IS', SUM
      END
RUN TWOSUM

  INPUT DATA  N:  5
  THE ASCENDING SUM IS  15
  THE DESCENDING SUM IS  15

RUN TWOSUM

  INPUT DATA  N:  100
  THE ASCENDING SUM IS  5050
  THE DESCENDING SUM IS  5050
```

PRINT *, 'J =', J, ' SUM =', SUM

RUN TWOSUM

INPUT DATA   N: 5
J = 1   SUM = 1
J = 2   SUM = 3
J = 3   SUM = 6
J = 4   SUM = 10
J = 5   SUM = 15
THE ASCENDING SUM IS 15
THE DESCENDING SUM IS 15

```
RUN TWOSUM

 INPUT DATA   N:   5
 J =   1        SUM =   1
 J =   2        SUM =   3
 J =   3        SUM =   6
 J =   4        SUM =   10
 J =   5        SUM =   15


 THE ASCENDING SUM IS   15
 J =   5        SUM =   20
 J =   4        SUM =   24
 J =   3        SUM =   27
 J =   2        SUM =   29
 J =   1        SUM =   30
 THE DESCENDING SUM IS   30
```

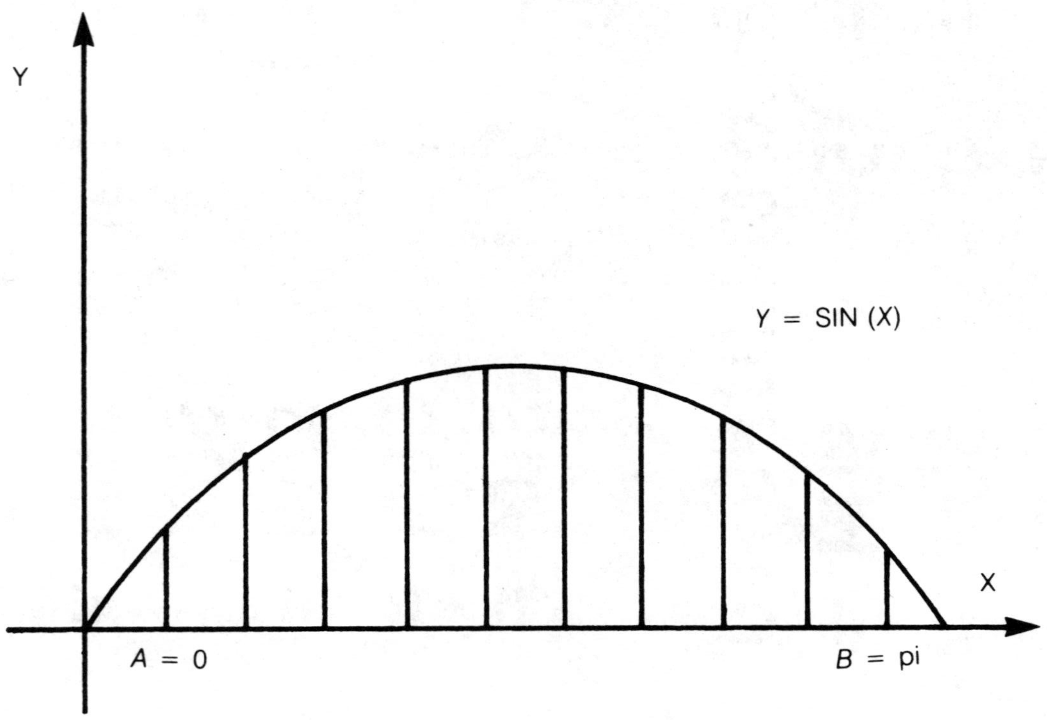

Figure 4.4 An area divided into n trapezoids.

$$T_n = h(\tfrac{1}{2} f(a) + f(a+h) + f(a+2h) + \cdots + f(b-h) + \tfrac{1}{2} f(b))$$

Subroutine:

General form:

> SUBROUTINE *subroutinename* (*dummyvariable*, ..., *dummyvariable*)
> *declarations*
> *Fortran statements*
> END

Subroutine Call:

General form:

> CALL *subroutinename* (*actualargument*, ..., *actualargument*)

Example:

```
      PROGRAM SUMS
      INTEGER TIME, N, SUM

      DO 18 TIME = 1, 3
         READ *, N
         CALL SUMMER (N, SUM)
         PRINT *, 'THE SUM TO', N, 'IS', SUM
   18 CONTINUE
      END

      SUBROUTINE SUMMER (N, SUM)
      INTEGER N, SUM, J

      SUM = 0
      DO 18 J = 1, N
         SUM = SUM + J
   18 CONTINUE
      END
```

Arguments:

Name: Gordon Grimswell
Semester: Fall, 1985

Class: 1989
GPA: 3.06

Course	Credits	Grade
Applications Programming for Turing Machines 105	3	B
Survey of Inca Music 321	2	A
Phrenology 294	4	A
Conversational Aztec 308	5	C
Precambrian Art & Architecture 220	4	B

Figure 5.1 A grade report for a student at South Mountain College.

```
      PROGRAM GRADES
C     FINAL VERSION
C     PRINTS GRADE REPORTS FOR THE ENTIRE COLLEGE

      CHARACTER SEMSTR *15, ANSWER *1
      INTEGER STUDNT

      CALL GETCOM (SEMSTR)
      DO 18 STUDNT = 1, 10000
         PRINT *, 'ARE THERE ANY MORE STUDENTS? (Y/N)'
         READ *, ANSWER
         IF (ANSWER .EQ. 'Y') THEN
            CALL ONEREP (SEMSTR)
         ELSE
            GO TO 19
         END IF
  18  CONTINUE

  19  PRINT *
      PRINT *, 'GOODBYE.  HAVE A NICE DAY.'
      END
```

```
C      SUBROUTINE GETCOM (SEMSTR)
       GET INFORMATION COMMON TO ALL STUDENTS

       CHARACTER SEMSTR *15
       PRINT *, 'ENTER SEMESTER AND YEAR:'
       READ '(A)', SEMSTR
       END

C      SUBROUTINE ONEREP (SEMSTR)
C      FINAL VERSION
       DOES REPORT FOR ONE STUDENT ONLY

       CHARACTER SEMSTR *15
       INTEGER MAXCRS
       PARAMETER (MAXCRS = 12)
       CHARACTER NAME *35, TITLE (MAXCRS) *25, LETTER (MAXCRS) *1
       INTEGER CLASS, CREDIT (MAXCRS), NRCORS, NUMBER (MAXCRS)
       REAL GPA

       CALL GETDAT (NAME, CLASS, TITLE, CREDIT, LETTER, NRCORS)
       CALL CONVRT (NRCORS, LETTER, NUMBER)
       CALL CLCGPA (NRCORS, NUMBER, CREDIT, GPA)
       CALL PRINT (NAME, CLASS, SEMSTR, GPA,
     +             NRCORS, TITLE, CREDIT, LETTER)
       END
```

```
      SUBROUTINE GETDAT (NAME, CLASS, TITLE, CREDIT, LETTER, NRCORS)
C     READS ALL THE DATA FOR ONE STUDENT
C     COUNTS THE NUMBER OF COURSES (NCORS) TAKEN

      INTEGER MAXCRS
      PARAMETER (MAXCRS = 12)
      CHARACTER NAME *35, TITLE (MAXCRS) *25, LETTER (MAXCRS) *1
      INTEGER CLASS, CREDIT (MAXCRS), NRCORS, COURSE
      CHARACTER TTLBUF *25

      PRINT *, 'ENTER STUDENT''S NAME:'
      READ '(A)', NAME

      PRINT *, 'ENTER STUDENT''S GRADUATING CLASS:'
      READ *, CLASS

      DO 18 COURSE = 1, MAXCRS + 1
         PRINT *, 'ENTER NEXT COURSE TITLE:'
         READ '(A)', TTLBUF
         IF (TTLBUF .NE. 'NO MORE COURSES' .AND.
     +       COURSE .LE. MAXCRS) THEN
            TITLE (COURSE) = TTLBUF
            PRINT *, 'ENTER CREDIT FOR THIS COURSE:'
            READ *, CREDIT (COURSE)
            PRINT *, 'ENTER LETTER GRADE FOR THIS COURSE:'
            READ *, LETTER (COURSE)

         ELSE
            NRCORS = COURSE - 1
            GO TO 19
         END IF
18    CONTINUE

19    END
```

```fortran
      SUBROUTINE CONVRT (NRCORS, LETTER, NUMBER)
C     CONVERTS LETTER GRADES TO NUMBER GRADES
      INTEGER MAXCRS
      PARAMETER (MAXCRS = 12)
      CHARACTER LETTER (MAXCRS) *1, L *1
      INTEGER NRCORS, NUMBER (MAXCRS), COURSE

      DO 18 COURSE = 1, NRCORS
         L = LETTER (COURSE)
         IF (L .EQ. 'A') THEN
            NUMBER (COURSE) = 4
         ELSE IF (L .EQ. 'B') THEN
            NUMBER (COURSE) = 3
         ELSE IF (L .EQ. 'C') THEN
            NUMBER (COURSE) = 2
         ELSE IF (L .EQ. 'D') THEN
            NUMBER (COURSE) = 1
         ELSE
            NUMBER (COURSE) = 0
         END IF
  18  CONTINUE
      END
```

```
      SUBROUTINE CLCGPA (NRCORS, NUMBER, CREDIT, GPA)
C     CALCULATE GRADE POINT AVERAGE (GPA)
      INTEGER MAXCRS
      PARAMETER (MAXCRS = 12)
      INTEGER NRCORS, NUMBER (MAXCRS), CREDIT (MAXCRS)
      REAL GPA
      INTEGER POINTS, CREDTS, COURSE

C     CALCULATE TOTAL GRADE POINTS
      POINTS = 0
      DO 18 COURSE = 1, NRCORS
         POINTS = POINTS + NUMBER (COURSE) * CREDIT (COURSE)
   18 CONTINUE

C     CALCULATE TOTAL CREDITS
      CREDTS = 0
      DO 28 COURSE = 1, NRCORS
         CREDTS = CREDTS + CREDIT (COURSE)
   28 CONTINUE

C     CALCULATE GPA
      GPA = REAL (POINTS) / REAL (CREDTS)
      END
```

```fortran
C         SUBROUTINE PRINT (NAME, CLASS, SEMSTR, GPA,
      +                     NRCORS, TITLE, CREDIT, LETTER)
C         PRINT GRADE REPORT FOR ONE STUDENT
          CHARACTER NAME *35, SEMSTR *15
          REAL GPA
          INTEGER MAXCRS
          PARAMETER (MAXCRS = 12)
          INTEGER CLASS, NRCORS, CREDIT (MAXCRS), COURSE
          CHARACTER TITLE (MAXCRS) *25, LETTER (MAXCRS) *1

          PRINT *
          PRINT '(A, A, T40, A, I4)', 'NAME:   ', NAME, 'CLASS:   ', CLASS
          PRINT '(A, A, T40, A, F6.2)',
      +        'SEMESTER AND YEAR:   ', SEMSTR, 'GPA:   ', GPA
          PRINT *
          PRINT '(A15, A30, A15)', 'COURSE', 'CREDIT', 'GRADE'

          DO 18 COURSE = 1, NRCORS
              PRINT '(A25, I18, A15)',
      +            TITLE (COURSE), CREDIT (COURSE), LETTER (COURSE)
18        CONTINUE

          PRINT *
          END
```

```
RUN GRADES

    ENTER SEMESTER AND YEAR:
    FALL 1985
    ARE THERE ANY MORE STUDENTS? (Y/N)
    Y
    ENTER STUDENT'S NAME:
    GORDON GRIMSWELL
    ENTER STUDENT'S GRADUATING CLASS:
    1989
    ENTER NEXT COURSE TITLE:
    PROG. TURING MACHINES 105
    ENTER CREDIT FOR THIS COURSE:
    3
    ENTER LETTER GRADE FOR THIS COURSE:
    B
    ENTER NEXT COURSE TITLE:
    SURVEY OF INCA MUSIC 321
    ENTER CREDIT FOR THIS COURSE:
    2
    ENTER LETTER GRADE FOR THIS COURSE:
    A
    ENTER NEXT COURSE TITLE:
    PHRENOLOGY 294
    ENTER CREDIT FOR THIS COURSE:
    4
    ENTER LETTER GRADE FOR THIS COURSE:
    A
```

```
ENTER NEXT COURSE TITLE:
CONVERSATIONAL AZTEC 308
ENTER CREDIT FOR THIS COURSE:
5
ENTER LETTER GRADE FOR THIS COURSE:
C
ENTER NEXT COURSE TITLE:
PRECAMBRIAN ART ARCH. 220
ENTER CREDIT FOR THIS COURSE:
4
ENTER LETTER GRADE FOR THIS COURSE:
B
ENTER NEXT COURSE TITLE:
NO MORE COURSES
```

| NAME: GORDON GRIMSWELL | CLASS: 1989 |
| SEMESTER AND YEAR: FALL 1985 | GPA: 3.06 |

COURSE	CREDIT	GRADE
PROG. TURING MACHINES 105	3	B
SURVEY OF INCA MUSIC 321	2	A
PHRENOLOGY 294	4	A
CONVERSATIONAL AZTEC 308	5	C
PRECAMBRIAN ART ARCH. 220	4	B

```
ARE THERE ANY MORE STUDENTS? (Y/N)
Y
```

```
PROGRAM PROPER
    .
    .
    .
READ (...) X, Y

IF (X .GT. Y) THEN
    CALL SWAPI (X, Y)
END IF
    .
    .
    .
```

```
                          X   Y
SUBROUTINE SWAPI (A, B)
                  X   Y
INTEGER A, B, TEMP
              X
TEMP = A
       X   Y
A = B
       X
B = TEMP
END
```

Figure 5.5 Supplying arguments to a subroutine.

```
      SUBROUTINE READLI (LIST, MAXSUB, SIGNAL, COUNT)
C     READ A LIST OF INTEGERS
C     STOP WHEN THE VALUE SIGNAL IS READ,
C     AND RETURN THE COUNT

      INTEGER LIST (1 : MAXSUB), SIGNAL, COUNT, I, BUFFER

      DO 18 I = 1, MAXSUB
         READ *, BUFFER
         PRINT *, 'INPUT DATA BUFFER:', BUFFER
         IF (BUFFER .NE. SIGNAL) THEN
            LIST (I) = BUFFER
            COUNT = I
         ELSE
            GO TO 19
         END IF
18    CONTINUE
19    END
```

```
      SUBROUTINE PRNTLI (LIST, COUNT)
C     PRINT A LIST OF INTEGERS

      INTEGER LIST (1 : COUNT), COUNT, I

      DO 18 I = 1, COUNT
         PRINT *, LIST (I)
   18 CONTINUE
      END
```

C
```
FUNCTION ROUND (NUMBER, PRECSN)
                   6.789    0.1
ROUNDS NUMBER TO GIVEN PRECISION
REAL ROUND, NUMBER, PRECSN
INTEGER WHOLE
              6.789    0.1
WHOLE = NINT (NUMBER / PRECSN)
                      0.1
ROUND = WHOLE * PRECSN
END
```

Figure 5.7 Supplying arguments to a function program.

```fortran
      I = 1
      PRINT *, LSTCRD (I)
      I = 2
      PRINT *, LSTCRD (I)
      I = 3
      PRINT *, LSTCRD (I)


      PRINT *, LSTCRD (1)
      PRINT *, LSTCRD (2)
      PRINT *, LSTCRD (3)


      SUBROUTINE PRTLST (LSTCRD)
      INTEGER LSTCRD (1 : 8262)
      INTEGER I

      DO 18 I = 1, 8262
          PRINT *, LSTCRD (I)
 18   CONTINUE
      END
```

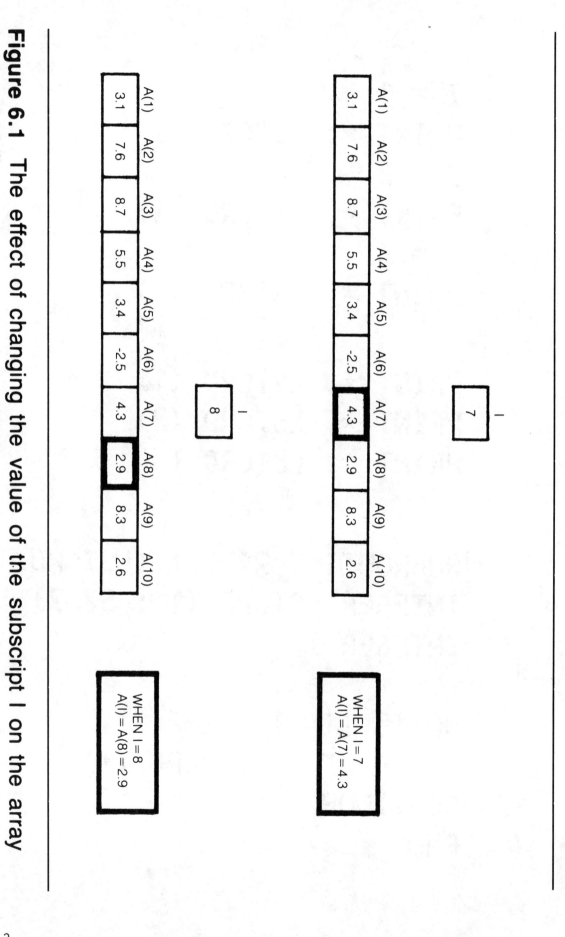

Figure 6.1 The effect of changing the value of the subscript I on the array element A (I).

```
      PROGRAM VECSUM
      INTEGER SIZE
      PARAMETER (SIZE = 3)
      INTEGER A (1 : SIZE), B (1 : SIZE), C (1 : SIZE), I

      PRINT *, 'INPUT DATA', SIZE, 'COMPONENTS OF A:'
      READ *, (A (I), I = 1, SIZE)
      PRINT *, (A (I), I = 1, SIZE)

      PRINT *, 'INPUT DATA', SIZE, 'COMPONENTS OF B:'
      READ *, (B (I), I = 1, SIZE)
      PRINT *, (B (I), I = 1, SIZE)

      DO 88 I = 1, SIZE
         C (I) = B (I) + A (I)
   88 CONTINUE

      PRINT *
      PRINT *, 'THE VECTOR SUM IS:', (C (I), I = 1, SIZE)
      END
RUN VECSUM

  INPUT DATA  3  COMPONENTS OF A:
  1  4  9
  INPUT DATA  3  COMPONENTS OF B:
  5  12  13

  THE VECTOR SUM IS:  6  16  22
```

```fortran
      SUBROUTINE REDCRD (LSTCRD, MAXCRD, NRCRDS)
      INTEGER MAXCRD, NRCRDS, LSTCRD (1:MAXCRD)
      INTEGER I

      OPEN (11, FILE = 'CRDFIL')
      READ (11, *) NRCRDS
      DO 18 I = 1, NRCRDS
         READ (11, *) LSTCRD (I)
   18 CONTINUE
      END



      SUBROUTINE SEQSRC (LSTCRD, NRCRDS, CARDNR, FOUND)
C     SEQUENTIAL SEARCH

      INTEGER NRCRDS, LSTCRD (1:NRCRDS), CARDNR
      LOGICAL FOUND
      INTEGER I

      FOUND = .FALSE.
      DO 18 I = 1, NRCRDS
         IF (CARDNR .EQ. LSTCRD (I)) THEN
            FOUND = .TRUE.
            GO TO 19
         END IF
   18 CONTINUE
   19 END
```

```fortran
      SUBROUTINE SEQSR2 (LSTCRD, NRCRDS, CARDNR, FOUND)
C     SEQUENTIAL SEARCH OF AN ORDERED LIST
C     SEARCH IS TERMINATED
C     IF A HIGHER ENTRY IS REACHED WITHOUT A MATCH

      INTEGER NRCRDS, LSTCRD (1:NRCRDS), CARDNR
      LOGICAL FOUND
      INTEGER I

      FOUND = .FALSE.
      DO 18 I = 1, NRCRDS
      IF (CARDNR .LE. LSTCRD (I)) THEN
          FOUND = (CARDNR .EQ. LSTCRD (I))
          GO TO 19
      END IF
18    CONTINUE
19    END
```

Table 6.2 Binary search for the number 2415495 in a list of 16 numbers. An asterisk denotes the last entry of the first half of the segment still under active consideration.

Before any comparisons	After one comparison	After two comparisons	After three comparisons	After four comparisons	Given number
1096633	1096633				
1202604	1202604				
1484131	1484131				
1627547	1627547*				
2008553	2008553	2008553			
2202646	2202646	2202646*	2202646		
2718281	2718281	2718281	2718281*	2718281 ≠	2415495
2980957*	2980957	2980957	2980957		
3269017					
4034287					
4424133					
5459815					
5987414					
7389056					
8103083					
8886110					

T 6.7

Table 6.3 Binary search for the number 7389056 in a list of 16 numbers. An asterisk denotes the last entry of the first half of the segment still under active consideration.

Before any comparisons	After one comparison	After two comparisons	After three comparisons	After four comparisons	Given number
1096633					
1202604					
1484131					
1627547					
2008553					
2202646					
2718281					
2980957*					
3269017	3269017				
4034287	4034287				
4424133	4424133				
5459815	5459815*				
5987414	5987414	5987414	5987414*		
7389056	7389056	7389056*	7389056	7389056 =	7389056
8103083	8103083	8103083			
8886110	8886110	8886110			

```fortran
      SUBROUTINE BINSRC (LSTCRD, NRCRDS, CARDNR, FOUND)
C     THE VARIABLES FIRST, LAST, AND HALF
C     REFER TO THE PART OF THE LIST STILL UNDER CONSIDERATION.
C     INITIALLY, THIS IS THE WHOLE LIST.
      INTEGER NRCRDS, LSTCRD (1:NRCRDS), CARDNR
      LOGICAL FOUND
      INTEGER I, FIRST, HALF, LAST, ONLY

      FIRST = 1
      LAST = NRCRDS
      DO 18 I = 1, NRCRDS
         IF (FIRST .EQ. LAST) THEN
            GO TO 19
         END IF
         HALF = (FIRST + LAST - 1) / 2
         IF (CARDNR .LE. LSTCRD (HALF)) THEN
C           DISCARD SECOND HALF
            LAST = HALF
         ELSE
C           DISCARD FIRST HALF
            FIRST = HALF + 1
         END IF
   18 CONTINUE

C     THE ONLY REMAINING LOCATION TO CHECK IS FIRST ( = LAST)
   19 ONLY = FIRST
      FOUND = (CARDNR .EQ. LSTCRD (ONLY))
      END
```

Table 6.4 Comparison of Five Search Procedures Based on a 10,000-Entry List.

Search Method	Program Name	Comparisons		
		Minimum	Maximum	Average
Sequential search (unordered)	CRDCH1	10,000	10,000	10,000
Sequential search (ordered)	CRDCH2	2	10,001	5,001.5
Two-level sequential search	CRDCH3	3	201	102
Four-level sequential search	CRDCH4	5	41	23
Binary search	CRDCH5	15	15	15

Table 6.5 Comparison of Five Search Procedures Based on a 100,000-Entry List, based on most efficient partitioning of the list.

Search Method	Program Name	Comparisons		
		Minimum	Maximum	Average
Sequential search (unordered)	CRDCH1	100,000	100,000	100,000
Sequential search (ordered)	CRDCH2	2	100,001	50,001.5
Two-level sequential search*	CRDCH3	3	634	318.5
Four-level sequential search**	CRDCH4	5	73	39
Binary search***	CRDCH5	18	18	18

*Based on $316 \times 317 = 100,172$ entries
**Based on $18 \times 18 \times 18 \times 18 = 104,976$ entries
***Based on $2^{17} = 131,072$ entries

```
      PROGRAM RANKLU
C     PRINTS THE NAME OF THE PERSON
C     WITH A GIVEN RANK IN THE CLASS

      CHARACTER NAME (1 : 10) *20
      INTEGER RANK (1 : 10), I, INRANK

      DATA NAME / 'AARON AARDVARK', 'BETTY BANANA',
     +            'CHARLES CANARY', 'DOLORES DONUT',
     +            'EDGAR ELEPHANT', 'FREDERICK FARKLE',
     +            'GRETA GIRAFFE', 'HARRY HIPPOPOTAMUS',
     +            'ICHOBOD IGLOO', 'JASON JACKRABBIT' /
      DATA RANK / 2, 7, 3, 1, 5, 10, 3, 9, 6, 8 /

      PRINT *, 'ENTER RANK IN THE GRADUATING CLASS'
      READ *, INRANK

C     SEARCH FOR THE GIVEN RANK
      DO 18 I = 1, 10
         IF (INRANK .EQ. I) THEN
            PRINT *, 'THE PERSON RANKING', INRANK,
     +               'IN THE CLASS IS', NAME (I)
         END IF
  18  CONTINUE
      END
RUN RANKLU

  ENTER RANK IN THE GRADUATING CLASS
5
  THE PERSON RANKING  5  IN THE CLASS IS  EDGAR ELEPHANT
```

T 6.10

```fortran
      OPEN (UNIT = 11, FILE = 'DATA',
     +      ACCESS = 'SEQUENTIAL', STATUS = 'OLD')

      OPEN (11, FILE = 'DATA',
     +      ACCESS = 'SEQUENTIAL', STATUS = 'OLD')


      READ (11, *) A, B, C

      WRITE (11, *) A, B, C

      REWIND (UNIT = 11)

      OPEN (UNIT = 12, FILE = 'DFILE',
     +      ACCESS = 'DIRECT', RECL = 20)
      WRITE (12, REC = 1) A
      WRITE (12, REC = 3) D
      WRITE (12, REC = 5) G
      WRITE (12, REC = 2) R
      READ (12, REC = 3) X

      CLOSE (UNIT = 12)
```

```
C       PROGRAM UPDATE
        THIS PROGRAM UPDATES THE LITTLE BLACK BOOK
        INTEGER MAXENT, MANY, NAMLEN
        PARAMETER (MAXENT = 100, MANY = 1000, NAMLEN = 20)
        CHARACTER NAME (100) *(NAMLEN)
        INTEGER PHONE (100)
        INTEGER NRENT, CHANGE
        CHARACTER REQEST *6

        CALL READBK (NAME, PHONE, MAXENT, NRENT)
        DO 18 CHANGE = 1, MANY
           PRINT *, 'ENTER A REQUEST:'
           READ '(A)', REQEST
           IF (REQEST .EQ. 'ADD') THEN
              CALL ADD (NAME, PHONE, MAXENT, NRENT)
           ELSE IF (REQEST .EQ. 'DELETE') THEN
              CALL DELETE (NAME, PHONE, NRENT)
           ELSE IF (REQEST .EQ. 'DONE') THEN
              GO TO 19
           ELSE
              PRINT *, 'REQUEST MUST BE "ADD", "DELETE", OR "DONE"'
           END IF
18      CONTINUE
19      CALL WRITBK (NAME, PHONE, NRENT)
        END
```

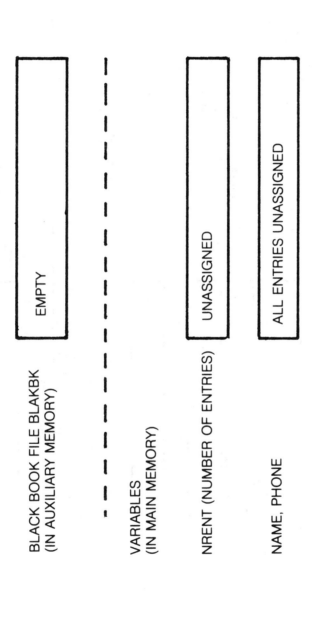

Figure 7.4 The empty black book file (in auxiliary memory) and values (as yet unassigned) of the arrays NAME and PHONE (in main memory) at the start of an execution of the program UPDATE.

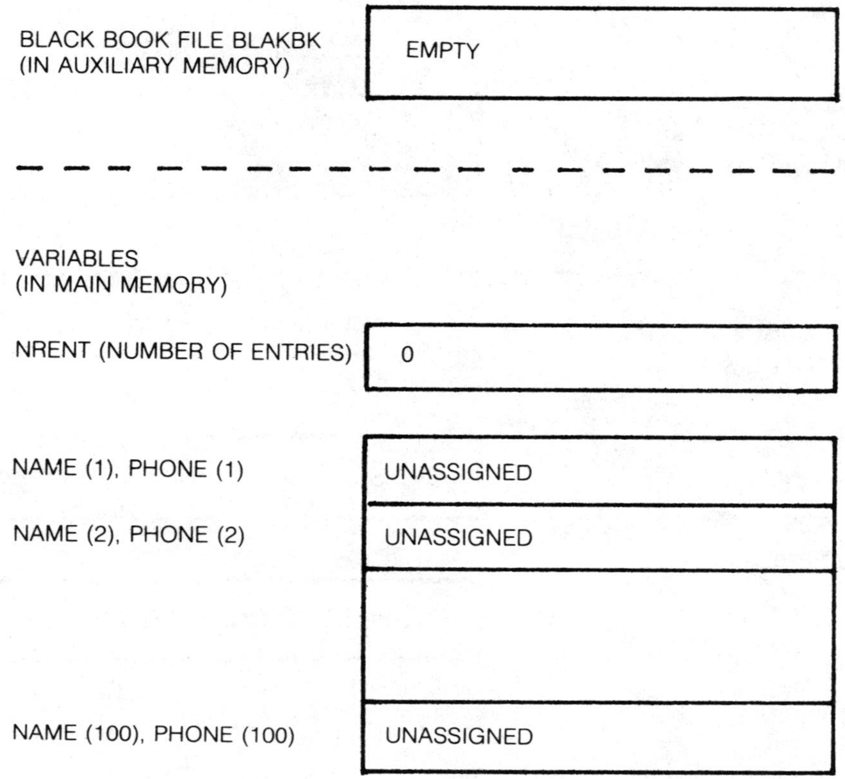

BLACK BOOK FILE BLAKBK
(IN AUXILIARY MEMORY)

| EMPTY |

VARIABLES
(IN MAIN MEMORY)

NRENT (NUMBER OF ENTRIES)

| 0 |

NAME (1), PHONE (1)

| UNASSIGNED |

NAME (2), PHONE (2)

| UNASSIGNED |

NAME (100), PHONE (100)

| UNASSIGNED |

Figure 7.5 The empty black book file and values of the arrays NAME and PHONE after reading contents of the black book file from auxiliary memory into main memory.

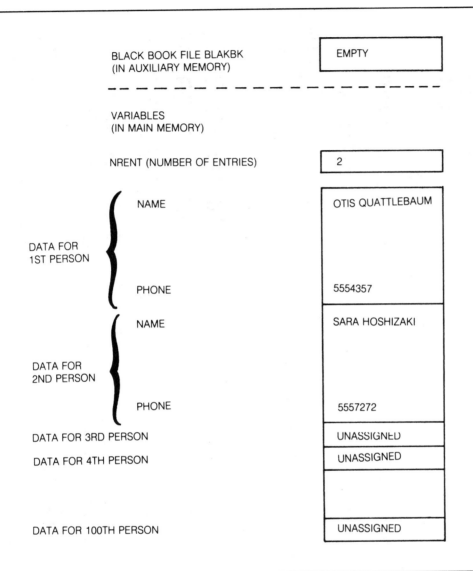

BLACK BOOK FILE BLAKBK
(IN AUXILIARY MEMORY)

EMPTY

VARIABLES
(IN MAIN MEMORY)

NRENT (NUMBER OF ENTRIES)   2

DATA FOR
1ST PERSON
{ NAME   OTIS QUATTLEBAUM
  PHONE   5554357

DATA FOR
2ND PERSON
{ NAME   SARA HOSHIZAKI
  PHONE   5557272

DATA FOR 3RD PERSON   UNASSIGNED

DATA FOR 4TH PERSON   UNASSIGNED

DATA FOR 100TH PERSON   UNASSIGNED

Figure 7.6 The empty black book file and values of the arrays NAME and PHONE after data for the Quattlebaum and Hoshizaki entries are read. The braces indicate a conceptual organization of the data into groups of related items.

```
      SUBROUTINE READBK (NAME, PHONE, MAXENT, NRENT)
C     READ IN THE CONTENTS OF THE BLACK BOOK,
C     NOTING THE NUMBER OF ENTRIES, NRENT
      INTEGER MAXENT, NRENT
      CHARACTER NAME (MAXENT) *(*)
      INTEGER PHONE (MAXENT)
      INTEGER ENTRY

      OPEN (UNIT = 1, FILE = 'BLAKBK', STATUS = 'OLD')
      REWIND (UNIT = 1)
      DO 18 ENTRY = 1, MAXENT
         READ (UNIT = 1, '(A20, I7)', END = 19)
   +        NAME (ENTRY), PHONE (ENTRY)
18    CONTINUE
19    NRENT = ENTRY - 1
      END
```

BLACK BOOK FILE BLAKBK
(IN AUXILIARY MEMORY)

OTIS QUATTLEBAUM 5554357
SARA HOSHIZAKI 5557272

VARIABLES
(IN MAIN MEMORY)

NRENT (NUMBER OF ENTRIES)

2

DATA FOR 1ST PERSON

DATA FOR 2ND PERSON

DATA FOR 3RD PERSON

DATA FOR 4TH PERSON

OTIS QUATTLEBAUM 5554357
SARA HOSHIZAKI 5557272
UNASSIGNED
UNASSIGNED

DATA FOR 100TH PERSON

UNASSIGNED

Figure 7.7 Contents of black book file and values of NAME and PHONE after rewriting the auxiliary memory file. Values in main memory are lost after program termination, but values in the auxiliary memory file BLAKBK are retained for later use.

```
BLACK BOOK FILE BLAKBK          OTIS QUATTLEBAUM. . .
(IN AUXILIARY MEMORY)
                                SARA HOSHIZAKI. . .


— — — — — — — — — — — — — — — — — — — —


VARIABLES
(IN MAIN MEMORY)


NRENT (NUMBER OF ENTRIES)       4


NAME (1). . .                   OTIS QUATTLEBAUM. . .

NAME (2). . .                   SARA HOSHIZAKI. . .

NAME (3). . .                   PEGGEE FRANKLIN. . .

NAME (4). . .                   CAROLE HICKE. . .

NAME (5). . .                   UNASSIGNED

NAME (6). . .                   UNASSIGNED



NAME (100). . .                 UNASSIGNED
```

Figure 7.8 Contents of black book file and values of the arrays NAME and PHONE after two more entries are added to the main memory copy of the file.

BLACK BOOK FILE BLAKBK
(IN AUXILIARY MEMORY)

OTIS QUATTLEBAUM...
SARA HOSHIZAKI...

- -

VARIABLES
(IN MAIN MEMORY)

NRENT (NUMBER OF ENTRIES)

3

NAME (1)...	OTIS QUATTLEBAUM...
NAME (2)...	SARA HOSHIZAKI...
NAME (3)...	CAROLE HICKE...
NAME (4)...	PEGGEE FRANKLIN...
NAME (5)...	UNASSIGNED
NAME (6)...	UNASSIGNED
NAME (100)...	UNASSIGNED

Figure 7.9 Contents of black book file and values of the arrays NAME and PHONE after the entry for Sara Hoshizaki is deleted. The duplicate entry for Carole Hicke has no effect on the program because the value of NRENT is 3.

BLACK BOOK FILE BLAKBK
(IN AUXILIARY MEMORY)

OTIS QUATTLEBAUM. . .
SARA HOSHIZAKI. . .
PEGGEE FRANKLIN. . .

- -

VARIABLES
(IN MAIN MEMORY)

NRENT (NUMBER OF ENTRIES)

3

NAME (1). . .	OTIS QUATTLEBAUM. . .
NAME (2). . .	CAROLE HICKE. . .
NAME (3). . .	PEGGEE FRANKLIN. . .
NAME (4). . .	CAROLE HICKE. . .
NAME (5). . .	UNASSIGNED
NAME (6). . .	UNASSIGNED
NAME (100). . .	UNASSIGNED

Figure 7.10 Contents of black book file and values of the arrays NAME and PHONE after execution of the subroutine WRITBK. Values in main memory will be lost at the conclusion of the execution of UPDATE, but values recorded in the auxiliary memory file BLAKBK preserve the information for future use.

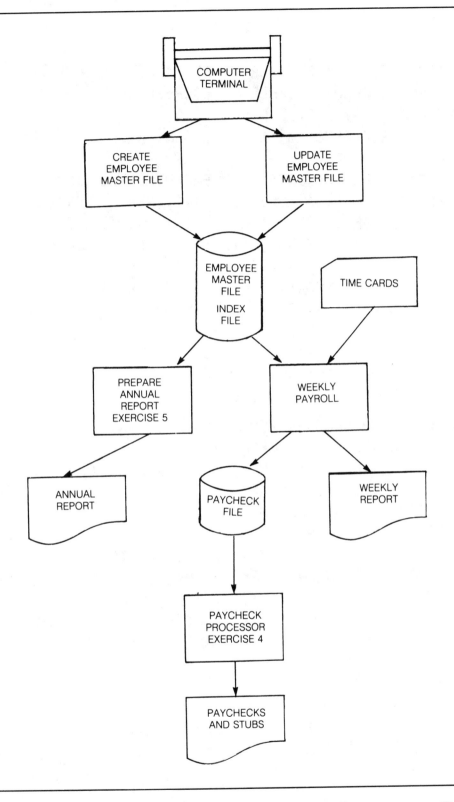

Figure 7.11 Flow of information in the payroll system. Rectangles represent programs and cylinders represent direct-access files.

```
C         REFINEMENT OF THE MAJOR IF BLOCK OF THE PROGRAM WEEKLY
C         DETERMINE RECORD NUMBER OF CORRESPONDING
C         EMPLOYEE MASTER FILE RECORD
          CALL LOCREC (SSNTAB, NREMPS, SSN, RECNUM, FOUND)
          IF (FOUND) THEN
C             READ EMPLOYEE DATA FROM EMPLOYEE MASTER FILE
              READ (12, '(6A, 5F10.0, 2A)', REC = RECNUM)
     +              NAME, SSN, STREET, CITY, DEPT, SKILLS,
     +              RATE, YTDPAY, YTDTAX, YTDFIC, YTDNET,
     +              STATUS, DATLST
C             CALCULATE INFORMATION FOR PAYCHECK AND STUB
C             AND UPDATE EMPLOYEE DATA RECORD IN MAIN MEMORY
              CALL CLCPAY (HOURS, RATE,
     +                     PAY, TAX, FICA, NET,
     +                     YTDPAY, YTDTAX, YTDFIC, YTDNET,
     +                     DATLST, DATE)
C             WRITE PAYCHECK INFORMATION INTO PAYCHECK FILE
              WRITE (13, '(2A, 8F10.2)')
     +              NAME, DATE, PAY, TAX, FICA, NET,
     +              YTDPAY, YTDTAX, YTDFIC, YTDNET
C             ADJUST TOTALS FOR WEEKLY PAYROLL REPORT
              CALL TOTALS (PAY, TAX, FICA, NET,
     +                     TOTPAY, TOTTAX, TOTFIC, TOTNET)
C             UPDATE PERMANENT COPY OF EMPLOYEE DATA IN MASTER FILE
              WRITE (12, '(6A, 5F10.2, 2A)', REC = RECNUM)
     +              NAME, SSN, STREET, CITY, DEPT, SKILLS,
     +              RATE, YTDPAY, YTDTAX, YTDFIC, YTDNET,
     +              STATUS, DATLST
          ELSE
              PRINT *, 'THERE IS NO RECORD FOR', NAME
              PRINT *, 'WITH SOCIAL SECURITY NUMBER', SSN
              PRINT *, 'IN THE INDEX FILE.'
          END IF
```

```
INTEGER STRLEN, MXEMPS
PARAMETER (STRLEN = 30, MXEMPS = 1000)
CHARACTER NAME *(STRLEN), SSN *11
CHARACTER STREET *(STRLEN), CITY *(STRLEN)
CHARACTER DEPT *(STRLEN), SKILLS *(STRLEN)
CHARACTER STATUS *(STRLEN)
CHARACTER SSNTAB (1:MXEMPS) *11
REAL RATE, HOURS, PAY, TAX, FICA, NET
REAL YTDPAY, YTDTAX, YTDFIC, YTDNET
REAL TOTPAY, TOTTAX, TOTFIC, TOTNET
CHARACTER DATLST *8
```

Variable	Format Specifier	Bytes	Type
NAME	(A)	30	CHARACTER *30
SSN	(A)	11	CHARACTER *11
STREET	(A)	30	CHARACTER *30
CITY	(A)	30	CHARACTER *30
DEPT	(A)	30	CHARACTER *30
RATE	(F10.2)	10	REAL
YTDPAY	(F10.2)	10	REAL
YTDTAX	(F10.2)	10	REAL
YTDFIC	(F10.2)	10	REAL
YTDNET	(F10.2)	10	REAL
STATUS	(A)	30	CHARACTER *30
DATLST	(A)	8	CHARACTER *8
Subtotal		249	
Future expansion		11	
Total		260	

Figure 7.13 Calculation of record length for the employee master file.

C = 'CRUNCH'

C (2 : 4) = 'RUN'
C (1 : 6) = 'CRUNCH'
C (4 : 2) is illegal
C (2 : 7) is illegal
C (5 : 5) = 'C'

```
        PROGRAM SGLLTR
C       PRINT INDIVIDUALLY THE LETTERS OF AN INPUT STRING
        INTEGER K
        CHARACTER STRING *10

        READ '(A)', STRING
        PRINT *, 'INPUT DATA  STRING:', STRING

        DO 18 K = 1, LEN (STRING)
           PRINT *, STRING (K : K)
   18   CONTINUE

        PRINT *, '====='
        END
RUN SGLLTR

  INPUT DATA  STRING:  SHAZAM
  S
  H
  A
  Z
  A
  M


     =====
```

```
      FUNCTION TRMLEN (STRING)
      CHARACTER STRING *(*)
      INTEGER TRMLEN, K
      LOGICAL NONBLK

      NONBLK = .FALSE.
      DO 18 K = LEN (STRING), 1, -1
C         OR UNTIL NON BLANK FOUND
          IF (STRING (K : K) .NE. ' ') THEN
              NONBLK = .TRUE.
              GO TO 19
          END IF
  18  CONTINUE

  19  IF (NONBLK) THEN
          TRMLEN = K
      ELSE
          TRMLEN = 0
      END IF
      END
```

```
      PROGRAM MULTT
      INTEGER MTABLE (1:10, 1:10), ROW, COL

      DO 28 ROW = 1, 10
         DO 18 COL = 1, 10
            MTABLE (ROW, COL) = ROW * COL
  18     CONTINUE
  28  CONTINUE

C     PRINT TABLE
      DO 38 ROW = 1, 10
         PRINT '(10I5)', (MTABLE (ROW, COL), COL = 1, 10)
  38  CONTINUE
      END

RUN MULTT

     1     2     3     4     5     6     7     8     9    10
     2     4     6     8    10    12    14    16    18    20
     3     6     9    12    15    18    21    24    27    30
     4     8    12    16    20    24    28    32    36    40
     5    10    15    20    25    30    35    40    45    50
     6    12    18    24    30    36    42    48    54    60
     7    14    21    28    35    42    49    56    63    70
     8    16    24    32    40    48    56    64    72    80
     9    18    27    36    45    54    63    72    81    90
    10    20    30    40    50    60    70    80    90   100
```

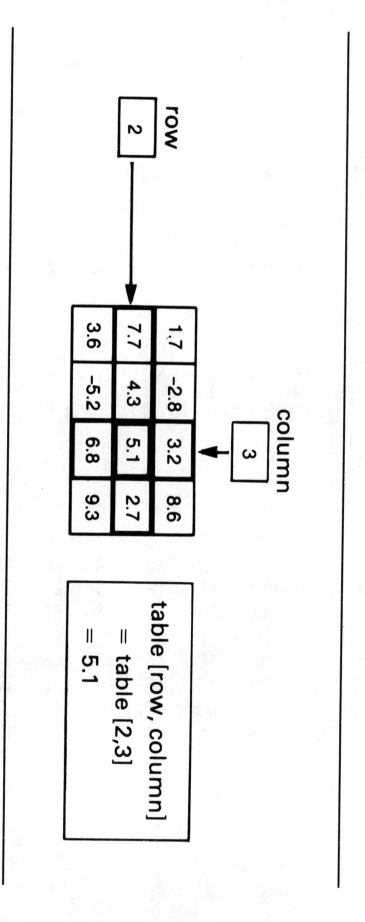

Figure 9.1 Referencing an entry in a table.

```fortran
      SUBROUTINE CURVE (GRAPH)
      INTEGER ROWMAX, COLMAX
      PARAMETER (ROWMAX = 10, COLMAX = 20)
      CHARACTER GRAPH (-ROWMAX : ROWMAX, -COLMAX : COLMAX) *1
      INTEGER ROW, COL
      REAL X, Y

C     PUT STARS ON CURVE
      DO 18 COL = -COLMAX, COLMAX
         X = REAL (COL) / COLMAX
         Y = X ** 2
         ROW = NINT (ROWMAX * Y)
         IF (ABS (ROW) .LE. ROWMAX) THEN
            GRAPH (ROW, COL) = '*'
         END IF
   18 CONTINUE
      END
```

RUN PRBOLA

GRAPH OF THE FUNCTION Y = X ** 2
-1 <= X <= 1, -1 <= Y <= 1

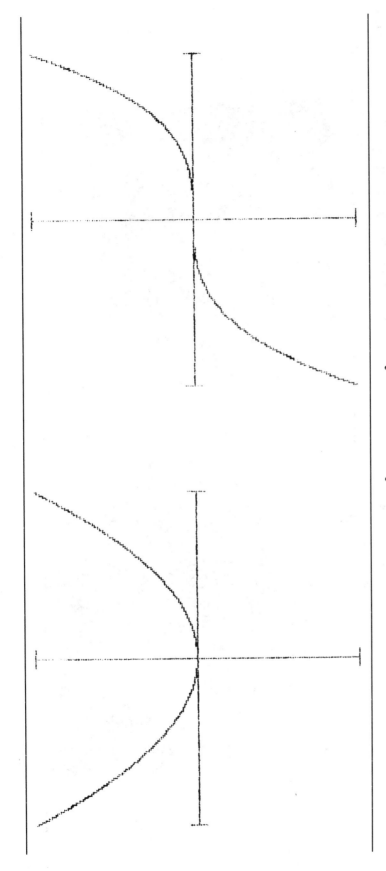

Figure 9.4 Graphs of the functions $y = x^2$ and $y = x^3$. These graphs were calculated on a grid of 191 × 191 pixels on a popular microcomputer and a dot matrix, higher resolution printer.

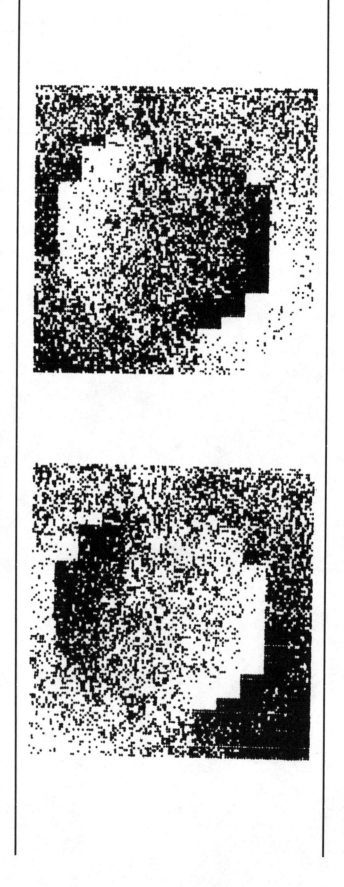

Figure 9.5 Digital image of a crater and the negative digital image of the same crater printed by a random halftone process.

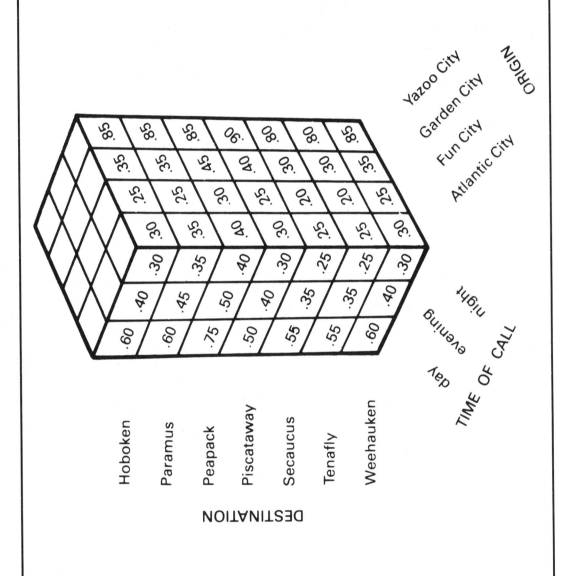

Figure 9.6 A three-dimensional table represented as a rectangular solid.

Figure 10.1 The environs of Mudville.

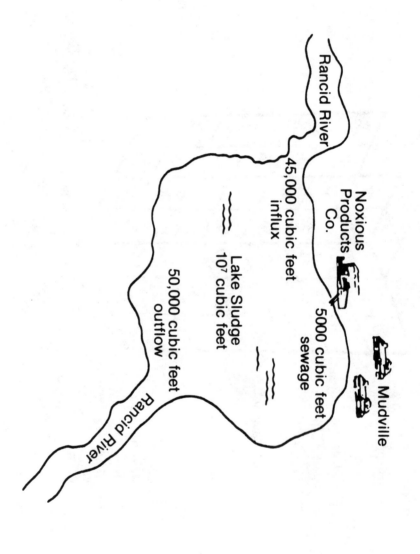

```
      PROGRAM DRILL
C     ONE PROBLEM, ONE CHANCE
C     UNREFINED VERSION

      INTEGER NAMSIZ
      PARAMETER (NAMSIZ = 20)
      CHARACTER NAME *(NAMSIZ)
      INTEGER X, Y, ANSWER

      PRINT *, 'HELLO, I''M A COMPUTER. WHAT''S YOUR NAME?'
      PRINT *, 'PLEASE TYPE YOUR NAME:'
      READ '(A)', NAME
      PRINT *, 'NICE TO MEET YOU,', NAME
      PRINT *, 'TODAY WE ARE GOING TO DO AN ADDITION PROBLEM.'

      Pose a problem, that is, choose two integers X and Y

      PRINT *, 'PLEASE TELL ME,', NAME
      PRINT *, 'HOW MUCH IS', X, 'AND', Y, '?'
      PRINT *, 'TYPE THE ANSWER:'
      READ *, ANSWER

      IF (ANSWER .EQ. X + Y) THEN
         PRINT *, 'CORRECT,', NAME
         PRINT *, 'VERY GOOD.'
      ELSE
         PRINT *, 'THAT''S NOT RIGHT,', NAME
         PRINT *, 'THE ANSWER IS', X + Y
      END IF
      END
```

```
        PROGRAM RNDDIG
C       GENERATES 50 DIGITS USING RNDINT (0, 9)

        INTEGER I, J, RNDINT

        DO 18 I = 1, 10
            PRINT *, (RNDINT (0, 9), J = 1, 5)
    18  CONTINUE
        END


        FUNCTION RNDINT (R, S)
C       GENERATES AN INTEGER IN THE RANGE R TO S

        INTEGER RNDINT, R, S
        INTEGER MAX, MULT, ADD, SEED
        PARAMETER (
     +      MAX = 1000,
     +      MULT = 21,
     +      ADD = 437 )
        DATA SEED /1/
        SAVE SEED

        SEED = MOD (MULT * SEED + ADD, MAX)
        RNDINT = R + SEED * (S - R + 1) / MAX
        END
RUN RNDDIG

        4  0  5  8  6
        8  1  3  3  8
        7  7  6  3  5
        1  8  4  8  7
        9  3  7  8  4
        3  4  5  2  6
        2  0  8  2  2
        6  1  5  7  4
        5  7  8  7  1
        9  8  6  2  3
```

```
      PROGRAM SVN11
C     SIMULATES THROWING TWO DICE
C     TO DETERMINE THE PERCENTAGE OF TIMES
C     A PAIR OF DICE COME UP 7 OR 11

      INTEGER ROLLS
      PARAMETER (ROLLS = 1000)
      INTEGER DICE, I, WINS, RNDINT

      WINS = 0
      DO 18 I = 1, ROLLS
         DICE = RNDINT (1, 6) + RNDINT (1, 6)
         IF ((DICE .EQ. 7) .OR. (DICE .EQ. 11)) THEN
            WINS = WINS + 1
         END IF
 18   CONTINUE

      PRINT '(A, F6.2)',
     +     'THE PERCENTAGE OF ROLLS THAT ARE 7 OR 11 IS',
     +     100.0 * WINS / ROLLS

      END

RUN SVN11

THE PERCENTAGE OF ROLLS THAT ARE 7 OR 11 IS 22.40
```

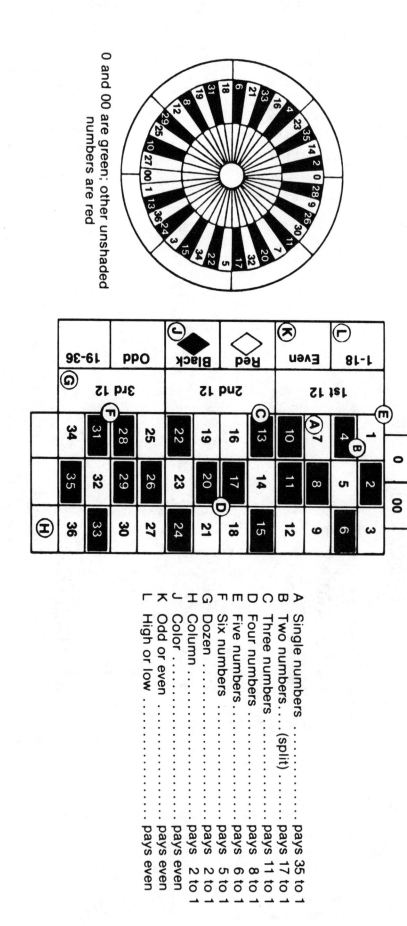

0 and 00 are green; other unshaded numbers are red

1-18 Ⓛ	**Even** Ⓚ	**Red** ◇	**Black** ◆ Ⓙ	**Odd**	**19-36**

	1st 12	Ⓔ		2nd 12		3rd 12	Ⓖ	
	1	**4**	Ⓐ **7**	**10**	**13** Ⓒ	**16**	**19**	**22**	**25**	**28**	**31** Ⓕ	**34**

0	00		3	6	9	12	15	18 Ⓓ	21	24	27	30	33	36 Ⓗ

A	Single numbers	. . . .	pays 35 to 1
B	Two numbers . . . . . (split)	. . . . .	pays 17 to 1
C	Three numbers	. . . .	pays 11 to 1
D	Four numbers	. . . .	pays 8 to 1
E	Five numbers	. . . .	pays 6 to 1
F	Six numbers	. . . .	pays 5 to 1
G	Dozen	. . . .	pays 2 to 1
H	Column	. . . .	pays 2 to 1
J	Color	. . . .	pays even
K	Odd or even	. . . .	pays even
L	High or low	. . . .	pays even

Figure 10.3 A roulette wheel and its payoffs.

```
      PROGRAM ROUFIX
C     SIMULATES A BETTING SESSION
C     AT THE ROULETTE TABLE
C     WITH A FIXED BETTING STRATEGY

      INTEGER NRBETS
      PARAMETER (NRBETS = 60)
      INTEGER MONEY, BETNR, WHEEL, RNDINT

C     START WITH ONE THOUSAND DOLLARS
      MONEY = 1000
C     SIMULATE BETS
      DO 18 BETNR = 1, NRBETS
C        PLACE BET
         MONEY = MONEY - 1
C        SPIN WHEEL
         WHEEL = RNDINT (1, 38)
C        CHECK IF RESULT IS RED
         IF (WHEEL .EQ. 1 .OR. WHEEL .EQ. 3 .OR.
     +       WHEEL .EQ. 5 .OR. WHEEL .EQ. 7 .OR.
     +       WHEEL .EQ. 9 .OR. WHEEL .EQ. 12 .OR.
     +       WHEEL .EQ. 14 .OR. WHEEL .EQ. 16 .OR.
     +       WHEEL .EQ. 18 .OR. WHEEL .EQ. 19 .OR.
     +       WHEEL .EQ. 21 .OR. WHEEL .EQ. 23 .OR.
     +       WHEEL .EQ. 25 .OR. WHEEL .EQ. 27 .OR.
     +       WHEEL .EQ. 30 .OR. WHEEL .EQ. 32 .OR.
     +       WHEEL .EQ. 34 .OR. WHEEL .EQ. 36) THEN
C           PAY OFF
            MONEY = MONEY + 2
         END IF
   18 CONTINUE

      PRINT *, 'THE AMOUNT OF MONEY LEFT IS $', MONEY
      END
RUN ROUFIX

  THE AMOUNT OF MONEY LEFT IS $  996
```